In Plain Sight

Reflections on Life in Downtown Eastside Vancouver

edited by

Leslie A. Robertson & Dara Culhane

Talonbooks
Vancouver

Talonbooks
P.O. Box 2076, Vancouver, British Columbia, Canada V6B 3S3
www.talonbooks.com

Typeset in Scala and ScalaSans; printed and bound in Canada by AGMV Marquis.

Second Printing: October 2006

The publisher gratefully acknowledges the financial support of the Canada Council for the Arts; the Government of Canada through the Book Publishing Industry Development Program; and the Province of British Columbia through the British Columbia Arts Council for our publishing activities.

Library and Archives Canada Cataloguing in Publication

In plain sight : reflections on life in downtown eastside Vancouver / edited by Leslie A. Robertson and Dara Culhane.

ISBN 0-88922-513-3

1. Women—British Columbia—Vancouver—Biography. 2. Women—British Columbia—Vancouver—Social conditions. 3. Sick—British Columbia—Vancouver—Biography. 4. Sick—British Columbia—Vancouver—Social conditions. 5. Poor women—British Columbia—Vancouver—Biography. 6. Poor women—British Columbia—Vancouver—Social conditions. 7. Downtown-Eastside (Vancouver, B.C.)—Biography. 8. Downtown Eastside (Vancouver, B.C.)—Social conditions. I. Robertson, Leslie, 1962– II. Culhane, Dara, 1950–

HQ1460.V3I5 2005   305.4'09711'33   C2004-903252-6

ISBN-13: 978-0-88922-513-8
ISBN-10: 0-88922-513-3

CONTENTS

The women who tell their stories in this book make the following dedications:

For my daughter.

I thank ATIRA for all the years you helped me.

I want to dedicate this to all of my friends—to Lexi, Francis, Jamie and Daryl, Shelley, Bonnie, Colsie and Carter, and, of course, Shari—the ones who were there when I needed them and still are.

For my "big" little brother who passed away too soon. I guess it's time for another change.

For my children Allen and Camille.

For Laurie and Lexi, the two best women in my life.

For those who will never walk a mile in my shoes.

INTRODUCTION

1. THE STORIES

You're looking at me but you're not looking at me. You're not seeing me.... We're here but you can't see us. You can't see the real us.... See, the buses come and go down here and you see people looking but they don't see nothing. All they see is the dope.

—Laurie

In Plain Sight presents the words of seven women who are publicly visible yet who, due to the blur of preconceptions that surround Vancouver's inner city, remain unseen.

To many, the women who live in the inner city (a community known as the Downtown Eastside) and who offer their stories here are "people without history," defined only by their presence in a neighbourhood branded by layers of stigma. Their individual perspectives are rarely included in the cacophony of media depictions of urban poverty, the "drug problem," and "prostitution," or revealed through statistics on crime and violence.

Here, women share stories of the diverse pathways they have travelled from childhood, into and out of the Downtown Eastside, through periods of addiction and recovery, strength and illness, affluence and poverty. Their stories confront the familiar stereotypes applied to drug users, to "wayward women," and to those who live with physical and/or mental illness. Our intention is to open a space for the voices of women who are seldom heard on their own terms, women who are highly visible on the street and in media representations but whose daily realities remain largely concealed.

In this introduction, we describe the process through which the narratives in this book were constructed. This preamble is also intended to acquaint readers with the daily circumstances and barriers confronted by the women who tell their stories. In order to provide further context to the stories, we then present a brief essay on the history of the Downtown Eastside, situating Vancouver's inner city neighbourhood in larger regional, national, and international processes. Recognizing that the narrators' terminology may be unfamiliar to some readers, we have included a glossary of terms as well as a list of acronyms for services and agencies mentioned in their stories. The narratives themselves are accompanied by two commentaries—

one written by the editors, and the other spoken by the narrators in which each woman reflects on the process of working on *In Plain Sight*.

From Interviews to Stories

Our relationships with these women began with an initiative known as *The Health & Home Research Project: Housing and Health among Low-income Women in Downtown Eastside Vancouver*. The first goal of this project was to understand how low-income women living in the Downtown Eastside define and analyze health and illness in the context of their everyday experiences. The second goal was to explore ways of doing research that would involve the women as both researchers and research subjects. (See appendix 1 for a detailed description of the H&H project.)

Initially, women offered anecdotes in response to such questions as: Can you tell me about how you came to be living in the Downtown Eastside? Would you tell me what a day in your life is like? In subsequent meetings, we focused on particular topics surrounding health and housing—topics that had emerged from previous discussions. We asked: Do you mind if I ask what drugs you use? When did you start to use that drug? Do you think it affects your health? How has illness affected your life? Who do you turn to for help when you need it? Do you feel safe where you live? What do you think women need in terms of health and housing? What are your visions of a desirable future? As we came to know each other, we moved from question-and-answer sessions to more open-ended conversations. Some women became keenly interested in reflecting upon and representing their lives and were enthusiastic about the possibility of eventually publishing their stories.

Each account in this book has been woven together from several tape-recorded interviews and conversations that took place between 2001 and 2002. They are social documents that record dialogues between narrators and listeners, frozen at a particular moment in time, in a particular place. As part of the creative process, researchers collaborated with each narrator to re-work their many interviews into a single, chronological account—an assembled text that condensed the many dozens of hours of interviewing and removed the (sometimes inept) questions, the awkward silences and flowing chatter; the coughs, intonations, and gestures. These compilations provided the starting point for the stories presented in this collection.

Editing and Compiling the Stories

The editors and narrators began work on *In Plain Sight* in January 2003, meeting regularly in diners on Hastings Street, cafés on Commercial Drive, and in the women's apartments and hotel rooms. During the first general edit, the narrators defined grammatical changes that would set the tone of their accounts. Some women wanted slang phrases and words removed; however, most of the narrators were adamant that their story should appear exactly as it was told. As editors, we strove to honour this goal: to present what they had to say in their own language, using the metaphors, explanations, and descriptions of events that they chose to speak about. We did not choose an editorial style—common in the work of journalists, researchers, and others—that applies a literary veneer to oral accounts. As a consequence these stories do not always flow smoothly, and it is important to keep in mind that verbal accounts are characterized by repetition, stutters, and hesitations that when read differ quite dramatically from more literary expressions.

Compiling the stories was complicated not only by the editing process, but also by the daily realities of the women with whom we worked. Their seven accounts emerge from under very particular regimes of silence that the narrators well understand; their speech is constrained by official and unofficial systems of surveillance; by sanctions governing how information circulates in the courts, through the media, and on the street; and by social stigmas attached to certain taboo topics. The storytellers are dependent on diminishing and fragile public services for basic subsistence: food, clothing, shelter, and health care. They live in a milieu significantly ordered by health and social services, wherein their narratives provide cues for diagnoses or for the implementation of policies that greatly influence their lives. By speaking of certain events, they risk legal repercussions as witnesses to or participants in illegal activities, and further risk the withdrawal of services and support from families, agencies, and government offices. Telling is a courageous act for women so vulnerable to the (mis)judgments of public and professional power.

The editing took place over several months during which the editors and narrators read and reread the stories together, adding and deleting as we worked. The women identified passages in their accounts that they wanted to remove or expand upon, and we began in earnest to edit the stories based on concerns for safety and privacy. We arrived at decisions about what to take out through conversations about particular events, the people who played a role in them, and/or the people who might recognize or be affected by them. For the sake of anonymity, we removed some of the rich particulars that distinguish individual women's stories. In so doing, we ran the risk of reducing the accounts to street memoirs, drug career narratives or personal histories of health and housing. To avoid this flattening of women's identities, we agreed to alter some details that may have unnecessarily identified them or their families in order to maintain as much of their individuality as possible.

Many women keep their street identities separate from their former lives. Personal stories are often dangerous to disclose in a neighbourhood where face-to-face interactions may be volatile and where, as many told us, trust is in short supply. Most women share the same community with people they identify as aggressors and abusers, making real anonymity doubtful. We did not seek to resolve contradictions in the stories, nor did we question or attempt to fill in gaps left by the narrators. For the sake of anonymity, some accounts exclude details about childhood and adolescence, or they exclude years of their lives they did not wish to make public. In other stories, women do not reveal the particularities of specific relationships, causes of death, or criminal charges. Such omissions signal boundaries of privacy drawn by the tellers that reflect risks to personal safety judged unnecessary by the narrators and the editors.

Our lives unravel in complex streams of dialogue that will never represent the rich volume of our memories, and it was difficult to draw to a close the ongoing conversations we had with the narrators. To some extent, budgetary and time constraints dictated the duration of the project. Mostly, however, the women decided when they were satisfied with their accounts and some chose to provide written addenda in order to bring readers into the present.

The women speaking here *In Plain Sight* are the subjects of their own stories. Believing strongly that they should have as much editorial control as possible, we recorded a concluding interview after each woman had approved the final form of her story. We chose to place transcriptions of these interviews as afterwords in order to be as true as possible to the process. Here, the narrators reflect on what the experience of creating their stories has meant to them. They explain why they want their stories made public, what they hope readers will learn, and who they hope will read them. The narrators' imagined listeners and their intentions in telling are important factors in understanding the stories themselves.

Most direct their narratives to those whom they imagine might be tempted by the "independence" of street life, by the seeming charms of exploiters, or by the allure of drugs. For some, their children and families will be important readers; often distanced and sometimes estranged, the tellers make special appeals to their relatives to read their stories and understand events in their lives. The narrators also address an ever-present public—those who are the current purveyors of judgment. While they are only too aware of the myriad ways in which they are excluded and marginalized by the mainstream—who imagine them as dangerous or exotic "others"—the women who tell their stories here include themselves within that public. One of the most emphatic points they each made is that they did not grow up wanting to be poor or addicted, dependent on illegal economies, on social and medical assistance.

During the final stage in our editing process, the narrators chose pseudonyms and titles for their stories; they then dedicated their accounts to their children, to members of their street families, partners, agencies, and community workers.

While we compiled the stories for *In Plain Sight*, we engaged in lengthy discussions with other researchers, writers, artists, community workers, and community residents about the risks involved in publishing personal narratives with little explanation or analysis. Their comments on the manuscript identified the need to address our editing decisions and to explicitly consider negative responses from those who may use our work to undermine the goals of the project. Few of us suffer quite as acutely if we are misunderstood and judged negatively, as the seven narrators in this book may. We discussed these concerns with the women whose responses we include here.

Our stories are told when something happens, when "the poor" or "unfortunate" meet with trouble, trauma, and tragedy. In shows and

pictures they show the most pathetic—they show us as this "thing"
and in people's minds, they're going to remember that. They don't
want to accept that we have a vivid reality.

—Tamara

On this occasion we were sitting in a café discussing with Tamara how some reviewers felt that we had not sufficiently protected women from the moralising scrutiny that their stories of drug use, troubled mothering, and illegal economic activities would elicit. She was surprised by the benevolent gesture but she was angered by the thought that such concern actually serves to erase the "vivid reality" of those people whose lives draw so much public attention. Like other women whose stories appear in this book, Tamara describes her life from a viewpoint at the margins, sometimes addressing the mainstream, but mostly concerned with conveying her story in a realistic and accessible manner. Our conversation continued:

In that introduction put down that we've been incredibly honest.
Things get covered up down here to pacify readers or onlookers, to
pacify those who want to believe everything is fine. Things get polished
a little to make it appear better when in fact it's not.

—Tamara

By turn, the narrators faced the quandary. Sarah was unmoved by the critique that making these stories public will further stigmatize the storytellers and reinforce negative stereotypes. As she told us, a discriminatory gaze aimed at drug use, poverty, and the sex trade more often than not already taints her daily interactions.

This is finally my chance to say something and for it to be accurate.

—Sara

To Laurie, the stories in this book are about survival and the celebration of that struggle—a hidden, difficult reality that requires exposure in this seemingly affluent society. Others like Pawz view their narratives as possible catalysts for the provision of services.

The government has already given us a safe injection site and they've
tried to give us housing but they need to know what's going on. If it's
not spoken about they'll never know.

—Pawz

Each narrator shared an understanding that she was revealing a concealed reality, a view from the social and economic margins that readers are challenged to witness and reflect upon.

Dialogues about issues of representation indicated a need to further sharpen the goals of this work. We decided to provide editorial introductions to each chapter. Our hope is that these will help to contextualize and, hence, to clarify the accounts as they were told.

Telling

In the face of layers of official and social silencing, the pride that these women take in telling their stories here should be recognized. Their narratives reveal not only individual hardships and defeats, but strengths and possibilities. Above all, they speak of survival and commitment to transformation. They express a desire to educate others and help those who may be drawn to life on the street. They emphasize possibilities, hopeful that their stories will reach those people standing at the delicate crossroad of decision-making. These stories encourage readers to imagine a sequence of events that could happen to anyone but that, in fact, happen most often to those whose choices are limited by colonialism, racism, poverty, sexism, violence, and illness.

When the narrators in this book speak about their lives, frozen portraits of "the poor" dissipate. Some women describe themselves as rebellious or ambitious, telling how the street appealed to their sense of freedom, how it seemed, at one time, to offer attractive possibilities. For most, however, the harsh independence of street life was imposed either by the need to escape physical and emotional violence, by financial necessity, or by illness and disability. Women acknowledge these circumstances that have forced them into a dangerous proximity to illness, sex work, and drug use. Once there, options for healthy living narrowed considerably. The narrators' work histories span professional careers and trade jobs; clerical, service, and domestic labour; activism, drug work, sex work, and many hours of community volunteering in exchange for small honoraria, food vouchers, or transit tickets. Financial strategies are complicated, and many women are generating income to support partners, children, and friends.

In the Downtown Eastside, street life has its own dynamic history, its own set of rules, languages, and social knowledge, most of which celebrate survival. In this book, the women speak a good deal about money, about how it circulates, and how they are able to generate a daily income. Anecdotes about the amounts they have made, saved, or spent reflect economic prowess that is highly valued on the street, as is the skill required to locate and obtain basic services. The women's daily routines include negotiations around access to shelter, clothing, telephones, laundry facilities, showers, and nutritious meals. Valued expertise includes the ability to perform effective cardio-pulmonary resuscitation, to manage relationships in the drug trafficking hierarchy, and to negotiate dangerous situations in the street-level sex trade. For the narrators in this book who are drug users, social knowledge extends to evaluations of drug purity and the risks inherent in particular practices relating to use.

In this collection of stories, some women describe lives ordered by addiction where the daily financial burden of buying drugs often eventually leads to participation in underground economies. Drug and sex work sometimes involve brief exchanges with strangers on the street, in bars or private rooms; at other times, women are embedded in long-term relationships with "regulars," "sugar daddies," and pimps, with people who perform various roles in the drug trade, from suppliers to dealers to those who work the street as "steers" and "packers." They are also connected to police officers and lawyers, many of whom they have known for years. They describe street ethics as continuously shifting in response to changes in the political and economic landscape. Some women are nostalgic for the "old days," and their accounts fill in the gaps of an ignored oral history.

The narrators in this book are attempting to move out of drug and sex careers, and their stories are testimonies that play a part in that process of transformation. Several women describe the pleasure, power, and excitement they initially derived from drugs; most recount how this eventually turned to self-imposed isolation and a sense of disaffection that often led to institutional support. One narrator speaks about her drug of choice as a long-term lover; others portray drug use as moments of reprieve from heavy realities. Some women convey the intensifying oppression of their dependency on the drug economy, of how addiction comes to define their work and their personal relationships; but many are ambivalent about the push and pull of their drug of choice.

Intended or not, there is a therapeutic dimension to the act of speaking about your life. Several women compared the research process to counselling, while others were reticent to engage in introspection. Clearly, the narrators speak from their diverse locations, but the stories reveal some common ground. Loss is a profound turning point in many of their lives. Loss of loved ones (through death or custody); the loss of meaningful relationships, a sense of belonging, or a physical home all hurl women into downward spirals. They describe either letting go or regaining their self-esteem due to important relationships, illness diagnoses, pregnancy, criminal convictions, episodes of violence, or periods of sobriety. External events such as the now infamous story of "Vancouver's Murdered and Missing Women" sometimes precipitate a swing towards recovery.

That so many women feel invisible and silenced in this community may seem paradoxical in the face of the onslaught of public attention to the Downtown Eastside in recent years. The most dramatic illustration of the simultaneous visibility and invisibility of women in the Downtown Eastside involves the story of the "Missing and Murdered Women." Since 1983 at least sixty-nine women from the Downtown Eastside have been officially listed as "missing persons." When their relatives and friends began trying to alert police and other authorities, they were ignored. As the numbers of missing women grew, and as academics, advocates, and journalists became involved and joined forces with women's families, "Vancouver's Missing Women" became a public issue, and the possibility that a serial killer was preying on the neighbourhood captured widespread attention. On July 31, 1999, the TV show *America's Most Wanted* aired a segment on Vancouver's missing women.

In February 2002, Robert William Pickton, a pig farmer from suburban Port Coquitlam, was arrested. He has since been charged with fifteen[1] counts of first-degree murder, making this the largest serial killer investigation in Canadian history. International media have flocked to Vancouver to film court proceedings and the massive multi-million-dollar search for evidence utilizing state-of-the-art technology at the Pickton farm. Families of the missing and murdered women and their supporters maintained a vigil at the Pickton farm, standing as witnesses. The interviews recorded for this book span the time before and after Pickton's arrest. By the time it is published, his trial may have begun. Robert Pickton is only one man. Women in the Downtown Eastside, particularly those who, like many of the narrators, live and work on the streets, say there are numerous men who commit acts similar to those Pickton stands accused of: men who come to the Downtown Eastside for the purpose of preying on the most vulnerable.

Just as poverty, drug use, and sex work are not unique to the Downtown Eastside but span in various ways all Vancouver neighbourhoods, so too the phenomenon of "disappeared women" is not unique to this city. Stories about large numbers of missing and murdered women—often marginalized, drug-addicted women involved in sex work—are being documented with alarming frequency around the world from northern British Columbia and Alberta to Mexico to Malaysia to Eastern Europe. Many of the women who tell their stories here live their daily lives in fear that their names may be added to the growing list of missing and murdered women from the Downtown Eastside.

Less detached observers than engaged witnesses, we ethnographers/editors of this collection hope to convey to readers of these stories not so much *information*, but *understanding*. We hope, first, to facilitate the narrators' *self-representation*: to provide for women whose lives and ways of telling may be very different from those of many readers, a space in which to talk about their experiences and their ways of being in the world, in their own words. Second, we want to serve as *translators*, providing bridges where necessary between the words of women living in Downtown Eastside Vancouver, and you, the imagined "average reader" who likely lives elsewhere, both spatially and socially. Third, rather than cataloguing "brute facts," promoting simplistic, formulaic explanations, or making grandiose authoritative claims, we attempt to render the creative processes involved in the construction of this volume transparent.

Finally, we hope this volume will contribute in some small way to our—narrators'/editors'/readers'—humanity.

---

1. In December 2004, Crown prosecutors announced that they would add seven charges and proceed to trial on twenty-two counts of first-degree murder.

2. THE PLACE

The women who tell their stories *In Plain Sight* are not representative of ethnic, occupational, health, or social communities; they are, quite simply, individuals for whom this work was important, for their own reasons. Shared place and time, though, does link them together: during the years they worked on their accounts, all the narrators who tell their stories here identified themselves as "Downtown Eastside women." Many readers, too, will doubtless come to this book with expectations constructed from other images, words, ideas, and experiences that shape what it means be a woman of the Downtown Eastside. This essay offers a broad overview of the historical and contemporary processes which work to create this locale, lived by some and imagined by many.

Boundaries demarcating the place now called the "Downtown Eastside"—including the name itself—and images depicting the people who live there have shifted significantly over time. Contemporary map-makers represent the Downtown Eastside as bounded to the north by railway tracks and the waterfront, to the west by Cambie Street and the downtown business and financial district, to the east by Clark Drive and the working-class and immigrant district of East Vancouver, and to the south by Venables Street and the Georgia Viaduct.

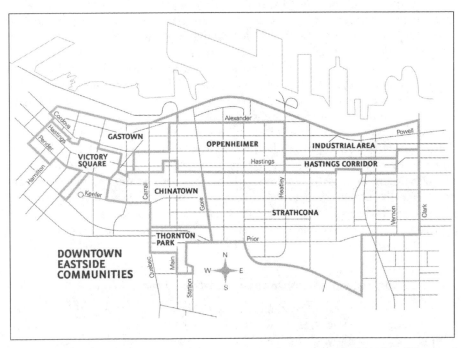

(Image courtesy of the City of Vancouver)

The Downtown Eastside is one of the poorest neighbourhoods in Canada. Average annual incomes hover below the national poverty line at around $12,000. Census takers tell us that about 16,000 people now live in the Downtown Eastside. Approximately 40 per cent are estimated to be Aboriginal, while 20 per cent are thought to be East Asian or Latino/a. There are small but self-conscious and self-identified groups of African Canadians as well as people from Eastern Europe, the Middle East, and Central and South Asia. Those remaining are Euro-Canadians, many of whom are elderly and disabled.

It is neither accident nor coincidence that a disproportionate number of people living in poverty in the Downtown Eastside are Aboriginal. The place we now call the City of Vancouver is constructed on territory held by Indigenous peoples of the Coast Salish First Nations for many thousands of years. Europeans arrived in the form of fur traders in the late eighteenth century and brought with them smallpox, influenza, and tuberculosis. Current estimates are that 90 per cent to 95 per cent of the Coast Salish population was wiped out by epidemics of infectious diseases over the course of the first 100 years of European contact. The Indian Act of 1876 allocated pieces of land, designated as reserves where First Nations were sent to live under the administration of government agents and missionaries. People who once knew what is now Downtown Eastside Vancouver by the Coast Salish place-name Luk'luk'i were relocated to these segregated spaces.

Some contemporary Aboriginal residents of Downtown Eastside Vancouver are descendants of ancestors who have lived in this particular place for thousands of years. Others have come from all over Canada and the United States. Some are members of families who were separated and dispersed by the Canadian government's infamous residential school policy. Some are individuals who have been shunned by their own communities' prejudices towards addiction, mental illness, sexual orientation, and HIV/AIDS. Many young Aboriginal people living on the streets in the inner cities grew up in government foster care or were "adopted out" and raised in institutions or by a series of surrogate families. However, not all the Indigenous people who live in the Downtown Eastside and other urban sites consider First Nations traditional territories or reserves to be their homes. There are also Métis, non-status Indians, and people whose families have not been connected to reserves for several generations. Still others positively choose, as have millions of people worldwide, city life. Challenging imposed foreign borders between on reserve/off reserve, urban and rural, some Indigenous people traverse the entire hemispheric space of what they call "Turtle Island" for myriad reasons.

A Brief History of the Present: Downtown Eastside, Then

Late nineteenth and early twentieth-century Vancouver developed as an industrial frontier town. Vancouver was the western terminus of the Canadian Pacific Railway (CPR), and Hastings Mill was built in what is now the Downtown Eastside. The sawmill and the CPR established the character of Vancouver as, very much, a company town. A bronze statue of Jack Deighton—owner of Vancouver's first saloon—marks the entrance to "Historic Gastown." The area's name memorializes "Gassy Jack" as a folk hero who represents the rollicking days of a wild frontier, a characterization given further impetus by the thousands of single men who moved into and out of Vancouver as they rushed to mine gold in the Yukon and northern British Columbia during the late nineteenth century.

Chinese men were transported to Canada as indentured labourers in the mid- to late nineteenth century to build the CPR, and Japanese fishers were brought to the west coast from their home country to harvest salmon. Chinatown and Japantown trace their roots back to this era.

Chinatown is no longer the residential choice of the majority of Vancouver's large Chinese population. However, a significant minority continue to live in the neighbourhood, and many more work and do business there. The border of Chinatown is now marked by a newly constructed ornate Chinese gate and by a giant mall and cinema complex, Tinseltown. During the 1940s the federal government confiscated properties and businesses owned by west coast Japanese Canadians, who were forcibly removed and interned in camps in the Interior of British Columbia when Canada and Japan were at war. A few stores and restaurants continue to operate on Powell Street in what was once called Japantown, and a community centre that houses a language school has been renovated on Alexander Street, but few contemporary Japanese Canadians make their home in the neighbourhood.

Dating from the early days of Hastings Mill the area was called "skid road," or "skid row," after the corduroy roads dug to slide logs into the water. The term "skid road" came to connote a uniquely west coast variant of a "slum" or "ghetto," characterized by a preponderance of hard-drinking, hard-living single men who, until the 1960s, formed the majority of the neighbourhood's population. Loggers, fishers, miners, and the members of towboat crews were often single men (or men living singly) who were isolated for most of the year either in camps or at sea. When they came to Vancouver during the off seasons many lived in waterfront rooming houses and spent their wages partying in the nightclubs, opium dens, bars, brothels, and beer parlours for which the neighbourhood was famous. Those who stayed too long, or those for whom alcohol and/or drugs became the focus of everyday life rather than a recreational activity, were said to have "hit the skids."

Beginning in the 1970s a new generation of community activists attempted to change the image of the neighbourhood by forming the Downtown Eastside Residents Association (DERA). Since then, the term "skid road," while still in common usage, has been rejected by neighbourhood representatives and criticized for being derogatory and stigmatizing.

Vancouver has also long been infamous as Canada's illicit drug capital, and what is now the Downtown Eastside—particularly the corner of Main and Hastings—has been the local centre of this industry, which was transnational long before contemporary pundits began to talk about globalization. Opium dens flourished in the early years of the twentieth century. Heroin entered through the port, and by the 1960s some cafés on the 100 block of Hastings Street were known as hangouts for heroin addicts and dealers. Local pharmacies conducted a thriving illicit trade in licit drugs such as benzodiazepines and barbiturates—uppers and downers. The neighbourhood became a destination for members of the marijuana-smoking and LSD-dropping youth counter-culture that sprang up across Canada and the United States in the 1960s and early 1970s.

Injectable combinations of prescription drugs like "Ts & Rs" (Talwin and Ritalin) joined heroin and powder cocaine during the 1980s, while crack cocaine—or "rock"—swept through in the 1990s and remains the hard drug used by many. Around 6,000 of 16,000 neighbourhood residents are currently thought to regularly inject heroin and/or cocaine and/or cocktails that mix combinations of legal and illegal drugs. The remaining 10,000 majority of Downtown Eastsiders are neither current drug users, nor drug sellers, nor sex workers. They are, for the most part, people who earn low incomes from poorly paid wage labour, social assistance, disability allowances, or pensions.

Illicit drug use and the exchange of sexual services for material benefits are, of course, not limited to the Downtown Eastside. Denizens of wealthier neighbourhoods engage in these practices as well; however, they do so in private homes and through brothels and escort agencies, their social power shielding them from the scrutiny of researchers, reporters, and police officers.

A Brief History of the Present: Downtown Eastside, Now

The corner of Main and Hastings Streets has recently been dubbed the corner of "Pain and Wastings." Since 1997, when the City of Vancouver Health Department declared a public health emergency in response to reports that HIV infection rates among Downtown Eastside residents exceeded those anywhere else in the "developed" world, this corner has become a focal point for emerging local, national, and international debates about the causes of, and solutions to, widespread practices of illicit intravenous drug injection and the spread of HIV/AIDS.

A global public has come to know the Downtown Eastside and the people who live here through journalistic sensationalism and the distancing language of academics, medical researchers, and law enforcement agencies. Two interconnected themes dominate public perceptions. The first focuses on exotic and shocking depictions of the illicit drug trade, commercial sex, and wanton violence and crime. The second focuses on promulgating implicit and explicit messages to the effect that the homeless (people too poor to rent or purchase shelter), drug addicts (people whose lives are principally ordered by drug use), and survival sex workers (people who rely on exchanging sexual services for money for basic subsistence) are lazy, deviant, and individually to blame for the impoverished and often brutalizing conditions in which they live.

Journalists, artists, and researchers most often represent the Downtown Eastside as a decaying and decadent urban spectacle. Cameras pan city blocks of boarded up businesses, thriving pawnshops, small grocery and coffee shops, single-room occupancy welfare hotels, drug dealers' turfs, and drug users' doorways. What the cameras fail to record are brightly painted wall murals and satirical graffiti; curtained windows, roof gardens, and flower boxes in hard-won social housing projects; and the schools, drop-in centres, clinics, missions, churches, parks, and playgrounds that announce that the Downtown Eastside is home for many—sometimes briefly, sometimes for a lifetime.

During the years that the stories presented in *In Plain Sight* were being told, the provincial government of British Columbia began an aggressive program to reduce public spending on human services. Living conditions worsened significantly for poor people in the Downtown Eastside. Young people from rural and northern regions of the province and from across Canada, discouraged by steadily declining opportunities for education and employment, and unable to secure affordable housing, continued travelling to Vancouver seeking opportunity, independence, and adventure, only to find themselves living on the streets and being labeled "homeless youth." During the summer of 2003 squatters erected—and were evicted from—tent cities around the neighbourhood, and young women continued to work on street corners around the clock. A police crackdown, entitled Project Torpedo, forced destitute drug users away from the entire 100 block of Hastings and onto streets and parks a few blocks away. At the same time, advocates and service providers succeeded in opening North America's first safe injection site for intravenous drug users, and an experiment in providing heroin by prescription to registered addicts has begun. Outpatient services for intravenous drug users and persons with HIV/AIDS, rejected by neighbourhood and citizens groups in other Vancouver neighbourhoods, have been concentrated in the Downtown Eastside. Tensions mount between drug users and non-drug users, between poor and homeless people and middle- and high-income homeowners, and between street people and business and tourist developers.

Questions surrounding the characterization and public representation of the Downtown Eastside are currently (2005) the centre of passionate debates. Political negotiations between neighbours, and between municipal, provincial, and federal governments, are being held to decide the neighbourhood's future. Like many contemporary urban spaces, the Downtown Eastside is a battleground where real estate developers, entrepreneurs, tourist promoters, artists, performers, community activists, long-time residents, newcomers, heritage house restorers and gentrifiers seeking character homes, police and health care professionals, 2010 Winter Olympic boosters, crime lords, and petty criminals vie for power. In what often seems a carnival of strange political bedfellows, confrontations and negotiations engender constantly shifting alliances, conflicts, and accommodations.

The future of the Downtown Eastside is uncertain. The stories told in *In Plain Sight* mark a moment in time and place. The narrators' voices inscribe the message that they were here, then as now.

Leslie A. Robertson and Dara Culhane
Vancouver, 2005

One

PAWZ
(For a Moment)

EDITORS' INTRODUCTION

"Back and Forth and Forth and Back" begins with an incident of domestic violence and a woman's relocation to protect herself from further abuse by her partner. Pawz recounts leaving work, family, and familiar surroundings out of fear for her life. She chose not to include information about her early life and carefully edited other details that could identify her to her aggressor, thus showing how his power to intimidate her crosses boundaries of place; he is still able to silence her voice. Her narrative also evokes the question of why it is victims of violence (usually women and children) who are uprooted rather than the perpetrators of violence (usually male partners).

Pawz describes her early impressions of the Downtown Eastside—a place chosen because of its affordable rent and the possibility for anonymity. She speaks about the continuing resonance of violence that she confronted daily, her shock at the openness of drug use, and her negative encounters on the street. As time goes by, and she begins to listen to other people's stories, she identifies herself as a member of that community and seeks to contribute constructively to it.

"Back and Forth and Forth and Back" was compiled from two interviews with the Health & Home Research Project and a follow-up interview in November 2003, at Pawz's request. It is the only story in this collection that retains the chronological sequence of the interviews. Perhaps more than any other narrator in this book, Pawz tells how, in their attempt to cope with poverty, people eventually accept conditions that they initially find shocking.

Back and Forth and Forth and Back

Edited from interviews conducted in October 2001, March 2002, and November 2003
Interviewer: Leslie A. Robertson

People have said to me, "I don't know how you don't have that fashionable white coat!" You know, the ones with the pockets in the back (*laughing*). It's because of all the things I've been through that have crossed over the line.

I had a child who passed away. I was almost murdered. I was raped. I've had all these bad things happen; yet I don't want to say I'm unhappy to be alive.

The nineties was a bad time for me. That's when my ex tried to kill me.

The cop told me, "I have to get you out of town. Today."

So they came to my house and we packed up whatever I could, whatever I had, and they snuck me out of town in the trunk of a car. The police relocated me to a safe house and I ended up moving to B.C. because my ex thought I would stay in [a different province].

I was starting over. Fresh.

I was in the safe house for two weeks. You have a certain period to decide where you want to go. I didn't want to stay where I was because he knew everybody that I knew. So I came here and didn't keep in contact with anybody.

I couldn't believe something like this had happened. I'd seen it on TV, but never in my wildest dreams did I actually think it would happen to me! I was in shock. I'd never had any kind of violent experience that I could remember. I had never been actually hit.

To this day, once in a while I'll be somewhere and I'll think that I've seen ————. And that fear comes over me—not fear but anxiety—and my heart starts racing.

I started thinking about things that I never thought about before—like retribution; I was planning it out in my mind. It started to scare me because I had never thought things like this (*laughing*). I went to a therapist, and she said to me, "What you are thinking is normal." As soon as she said that, I stopped thinking it because I realized that it was part of the process—the healing process. First it's shock, then it's pain, then it's anger, and then it's forgiveness. I found out that it *wasn't* me. I started thinking that maybe it was my fault, that I provoked it. I couldn't fathom the whole process, and still, to this day, when I think about it, I can't believe this happened to me.

I was in a transition house and one of the workers there, who was a counsellor, said, "You have to pick a job." I had to pick an industry where my ex wouldn't even think to look. I was going to do what I always did, but instead I decided to do something totally different.

I moved to the East End and started working for this auto-body company. I did my practicum and they asked if I would be interested in coming to work for them. I said, "Sure!"

But some weeks I might make major amounts of money and some weeks I might make nothing. I said, "I can't live on this!"

I told them, "I'm sorry, but I have to find another job," and I went to work at another company. It was good, but I have asthma, and being around all the dust and the fumes was giving me so many attacks, even though I wore my respirator religiously. I thought, maybe if I go on a part-time basis ... But nobody hires part-time. So now I have to do something else.

It wasn't until I came down here (*laughing*) that I really had an awakening!

Just the idea of Main and Hastings. Main and Hastings, with the cop shop right across the street (*laughing*). The amount of activity—they're so blatant and bold!

When I came here I was supposed to have a place with a friend, but they had already gotten somebody else, so I had nowhere to live. I needed a place quick and there was a hotel room that I saw. I ended up down at a place on ———. Of all the hotels it seemed like the best one—for a hotel or rooming house it was not bad. Not good, but not bad (*laughing*). I befriended the manager so that kind of helped a bit because he looked out for me. In the morning he would come and knock on my door and tell me that there's coffee in the office. He'd ask me, "Did you have any problems last night?"

One of the first nights that I was there, there was a knock on my door at eleven o'clock.

I said, "Hello! Who is it?"

A guy says, "Oh, it's me. Open the door."

I said, "Who is it?"

He goes, "You know—me," and he said his name.

I said, "I'm sorry, you've mistaken me for someone else."

He goes, "Just open the door!"

I said, "Come back in the daylight."

He said, "Just open the door."

I said, "Get the fuck away from my door!"

I didn't have a phone. I couldn't phone the police or anything, so I put chairs against the door. But it's not like in the movies where the chair props the door closed and it stays closed. The doorknob was here (*gesturing high*), and the chair's down here (*gesturing low*). It was just something to make me feel safe.

I told him, "I'm not opening the door. Get the fuck away!"

It went quiet for about fifteen minutes.

Then all of a sudden—I don't know what happened; there was all this banging and yelling and you could hear wrestling, and then it went quiet. About half an hour later I opened my door and peeked out and there was blood everywhere. I don't mean like just little drops, blood everywhere! I shut my door and I just sat against it all night long because I couldn't sleep.

In the morning, as soon as it started getting daylight and I could hear the birds start chirping, one of my neighbours was out there with a mop, just starting to clean. I said, "Don't! I want the manager to see this." I went and knocked on the manager's door. So he came up. He wasn't too happy about me waking him up that early, but when he came out he says, "Who was it?"

"I don't know," I said.

There was blood from the bathroom, all the way out the hallway, down the stairs and out the door. We don't know who it was, still to this day. I said to the manager, "I can't live in a place like this!" So they changed the locks on the front door and everybody had to start buzzing the manager to get in from then on.

But there was still the state of the hallway. You had to tiptoe through the syringes to get to the bathroom. I told the woman who owned the hotel and she said, "Ah, the manager—he'll take care of you. He'll take care."

Well, he took all the rent money and split that night (*laughing*). Some people didn't get a receipt. They said, "Oh, I'll pick the receipt up tomorrow." All those people lost out on their rent because they didn't get a receipt there and then. They had to pay again. I had mine paid directly from social services, so they couldn't say anything. Thank God for that!

In that hotel there were too many drunks and they started getting violent. There was one guy that was getting violent with his girlfriend, and it was really affecting me—and not just on a conscious level; I was dreaming about it. I'd see a girl with black eyes, and she'd say, "That's it! He's outta here!" The next day she's making up with him. I thought, "It's a vicious circle."

I only went through it once. You know, my parents have been married for a long time and my dad never hit my mom. You just don't hit somebody. And, if somebody hits you, you don't go back for seconds! I believe that. You don't deserve that; nobody deserves that!

And to see somebody say, "Oh, he loves me. I did it. It's my fault." (*Shaking her head*)

I don't believe in that. I don't believe that to love somebody you have to hit them.

So I would say, "You don't have to tolerate it."

And other people in the hotel were, like, "Oh, mind your own business!"

"Well, you're fighting and you're arguing in the middle of the night waking everybody up. It becomes everybody's business!"

I said to the manager, "Something's got to be done about this!"

I was supposed to take over the manager's job, but I started volunteering down here. When I told the landlord that I was *working*, she thought that I had a job, so she gave the manager's job to somebody else. That would have been a great job, being the hotel manager. Free rent, free phone; you work nine to five. All you do is clean up and collect the rent. Well, I was cleaning up anyways because I can't stand the dirt. It worked out to twelve hundred bucks a month and I worked out my food to two hundred bucks a month, so a thousand bucks cash in the bank! Every month! That's twelve grand a year, and the job was given to somebody else!

I stayed at that hotel for five months, something like that, but I was homeless for six months after. I found out about this new place they were building. I was volunteering, and a housing advocate told me about it. I ended up living on people's floors because the housing project said that they were going to be completed and then they kept prolonging it and prolonging it. First it was an earthquake, then it was budgeting, and they kept saying, "Oh, next month," so I couldn't really get a place (*sighing*).

My friend said, "Okay, you can sleep at my place on the floor."

I was between three friends, two days at one place, two days at another place, two days at another place. I was living out of a suitcase.

My friends were starting to get ... they'd say, "You said only a month!"

Two, three, four months go by and I was cleaning up everybody's place. I was buying my own food because I didn't have to pay rent, but my worker knew that I was only supposed to get support money. So I was cleaning three houses because everywhere I went I had to clean (*laughing*). Everywhere! My hands were getting sore, and where I was volunteering I was also cleaning, doing the floor. I was constantly on the go and I was losing all this weight. People were saying, "How come you're losing so much weight?"

"Well, I'm running around from place to place to place!"

And I couldn't sleep-in anywhere! If I wasn't tired I had to just lay there because my friends had to sleep (*laughing*). It was chaotic. When I finally did get in to the new place, all I wanted to do was sleep, and do you think I could? I couldn't sleep! I couldn't sleep! I was so used to that routine. The new place, there was a lot of drugs in there, and a lot of prostitutes.

One day I'm standing outside. I was expecting a friend to come over but I forgot to give them my buzzer number. I'm waiting downstairs, and I didn't know which way they were going to come from. So I was turning— I was looking both ways—and this girl comes down and she says, "Are you buying one?" I forget the actual words, "Are you putting out a buy?"

I said, "Excuse me?"

"Are you putting out a buy?"

I was, like, "What are you talking about?"

She goes, "You know ... are you looking for a date?"

I said, "No. A friend's coming over."

She goes, "You're a prostitute right?" (*Laughing*)

I was, like, "Excuse me! I don't think so!"

She goes, "So you're putting out a buy then?"

I said, "What part of 'I'm not a prostitute' don't you understand?"

She just looked at me and she started laughing. I'm thinking, "They're going to think I'm one!"

The first day I was in my new place, I had just had a piece of foam dropped off for a bed and an ambulance pulled up; a guy OD'd in the stairway. Well, you're right downtown and it's so convenient, when they want to get high they just go two blocks. I just wasn't anticipating that! I'm not totally ignorant, but I was ignorant of the lifestyle down here and how accepting it is.

I've had people come up to me and say, "Do you have water?"

At first I had no idea what *water* meant. "What do you mean *water*?"[2]

There's little blue things on the street and I wondered what they were. At first I thought somebody had lost something. Then I thought it was

---

2. Water is used to prepare heroin or cocaine for injecting.

perfume. Then it just clicked in; that's water isn't it? I wasn't going to stop and ask somebody.

You can't say hi to anybody here because the first thing they say is, "What do you want from me?" I lived in a small town, everybody says hi to everybody, and good morning. Out here, they close up, "What do you want?" I've kind of got my guard up now. It's been a wake-up call.

The whole coming-to-B.C. thing has changed me.

Living here, I think you become cynical and maybe desensitized? Have I said that correctly? Cold. I was never like that before. People would say, "Could I get a smoke off you, please?"

Now, I'm totally broke and I ask somebody, and they go, "No!"

Well, I've learned how to say no lately, and sometimes not by choice, just because I don't have. Even if I do, I've found myself saying no and it's kind of cold. It is.

I don't have money. I'm stressed. Because of my budget I don't have the right kind of nutrients, I can't buy fresh fruits and vegetables all the time. Welfare doesn't give you a lot of money! They only give you a hundred and seventy-five dollars to live on, and that's to pay all your bills too.

I got scammed down here. This chick—like, I don't get much money—and this chick came into the bar and she was bawling her eyes out. "I just got robbed! I have no money to get home!"

So I reached in my pocket and I gave her some money. That was a Thursday night, and I saw her on Sunday about one o'clock in the afternoon walking down the street crying, talking to this old guy. So I said to her, "Hi. Do you remember me? You just got robbed Thursday?"

She goes, "No! It just happened now!" The guy was handing her twenty bucks, and I'm, like, "Oh man! I got scammed!" She followed me up the street and had the nerve to ask me for more money. I was just livid! I just wonder how many people have dealt with that. How many people have been sucked into it? That's sad.

You know, you only have to go two blocks away and you can buy something for $10,000. If you come two blocks this way you can sell that thing for twenty bucks!

I'm learning a lot down here.

I think that women's most important health concern is physical abuse by men. Okay, let me rephrase that, by partners, by men and women. I think that's one of the biggest health concerns because I'm hearing it! I'm living right here on a daily basis and hearing it. Second, I would say, is stress, mental stress; and third, I would say is drugs—those three, maybe not in that order. Right now I don't have any health problems except for asthma and lack of sleep.

Almost everybody I know has hep C. Thank God I don't have it. I even went to the doctor's because—remember I was saying that I was homeless?—When I was staying at my friends' places, a couple of them had hep C. I was staying with three people, and two out of the three had hep C. I didn't know how it was passed on. Here I am, I'm drinking out of their cup, "Oh, there's a cigarette. Can I have a drag? Oh, can I have a sip of pop?" Same straw.

So I went to the doctor. I was really concerned. They tested me and, thank God, nothing.

I had the A and B vaccination (*showing a large scar on her arm*). Harsh, eh? I went once, then thirty days later a second time, and then six months later a third. That third one, I had nothing for a week and then it kind of bubbled up. They said, "Oh, it's just a reaction, it's fine."

I'm not a hypochondriac but I panic (*laughing*).

After my accident I started taking painkillers because of my back. The doctor said to me, "You know, there must be a lot of pain in people's lives."

I said, "What?"

He said, "For people to be taking drugs, any type of drugs. You must have some serious pain in your life to be taking these painkillers."

I started thinking about it. You can think of it metaphorically, whether or not you've had pain, whether it means, like, a broken heart or a broken bone. To be taking painkillers you must have had some serious pain.

I can't say that I haven't tried drugs.

But do I go and buy them? No.

In the seventies when I was going to school, I tried marijuana and all that. I've tried heroin, coke, crack, Ecstasy, MDA, and alcohol, of course. But I don't do needles or anything like that. Heroin and coke—I tried these in the last little while, the last year. I tried crack. You know, I don't live my life around it like some people who want it all the time. I prefer to have food and make-up and nail polish and, when I'm working, a lunch. I never do drugs on the street, always at a friend's house, and it's just because everyone else is doing it, kind of thing. I saw this thing on TV about being an addict—addictive. They had rats. I don't know if it was rats or mice, but they give them a hit of cocaine or whatever it is, and these animals who don't know the difference, they want it! I was in awe.

To see these people, they'll walk around with no shoes on their feet and totally dirty. They've given up! They've lost hope! What amazes me—or what I think about is—I look around and I wonder what's happened in their lives to make them get to that point. What has happened in their life? I look at drugs as a painkiller, and, basically, what they're doing is numbing themselves to the pain. Well, what was so bad that they have to keep themselves numb? Maybe I've got a few wires that aren't connecting, but you know, I look around and I think, "How can these people give up hope?" (*Pausing*)

I figure people are going to do drugs. There's no ifs, ands, or buts about it; they're going to do it.

I think it's a good idea that they have a safe injection site, not to promote drug use, but the fact is, people are going to do it. Now, at least you have the people there and you can say, "Look, this is what's available for treatment and recovery." At least then you've got their attention—even if it's only for a minute or two—instead of them just reading on a board, "If you need help call this number." They want help but they don't know where to go and what to do. This way at least you're giving them an avenue. I think probably everybody who's doing drugs will use [the safe injection site]. I think people are going to be curious. I mean, I'm curious and I don't even do needles.

I noticed that on all the four corners down here they have the different churches. One church gives out candy, bags of candy, and inside the bag they have literature from each church. You know, "Seek the Lord." So eating their candy is an incentive to get you to read their literature. Half of them don't even do that. They just take their candy and throw the literature away.

I think, legalize drugs. If they do legalize drugs—and over in Europe they have—I think within six months our deficit would be taken care of. Crime would go down to nothing because the criminals, I mean, what are they doing now? They're doing all this stealing and all for what?

For money to get drugs. If it's legal there wouldn't have to be all this crime, there wouldn't have to be the fencing.

Once in a while the police do a sweep but they've got to do something other than just that. They do it when something's going on—say, for the Molson Indy—then they do a big sweep so that the visitors don't see it. But as soon as the project is over it goes right back. Have more police officers doing the beat. Have something!

I get asked about drugs all the time, "Up? Down? Up? Down?"

All I do is, "No. No. No. No." You don't make eye contact.

I take the bus now. When I first moved down here I used to walk from the Sky Train, from Main Street down to Georgia. Now I'll take the bus. Just because of all the people out there that are not so nice. I get hassled on the street.

"How much? You need a ride. Get in! Come on, I'll give you a ride."

"No, thank you."

"Oh, come on! I'll give you a ride!"

"No, thank you."

"Oh, come on, I'll give you a ride. I'll give you a ride!"

If there was a cop I would have said, "Do something."

I've literally kicked a car. "I said no! What part of no." I was even going to put down on the back of my jacket, "I'm not a prostitute. Don't ask. Just don't talk to me."

Isn't that bad? Every night!

Just being down here—how can you say everyone down here is a drug addict? Or any woman down here is a prostitute? I tell you, I get so hungry some nights! I've thought about doing it!

I thought about it, but I can't bring myself to do it. I can't.

For women to be prostituting themselves, they've obviously got no respect for themselves. Or they don't care anymore. Maybe they do but they don't, maybe they have more respect for the drug. They'll do anything to get the drug, and I see that! It's like I'm looking into a fish bowl and I'm watching the fish swim around and I'm wondering why they keep on. Do they not realize? I don't know. But some people, that's all they've known in their life.

I got a letter from the government telling me to go to work or I'll get cut off social assistance. I believe it. It states that welfare's only temporary and that there are jobs available. Look! My hand is itchy. Money's coming! Oh, wait, that's the left hand. It's *right receives, left leaves.*

I liked working because I had something to do; I had somewhere to go. I was a productive person in society. I had money, and right now it's day to day, it's unknown. I'm still looking for work.

I have a friend and sometimes he needs help after he's completed a job, someone to go in and clean up the place. He'll throw me a pack of smokes or, if I need some cat food or something, he'll throw me something like that. A little bit of coin, not enough to—"Whoa! Let's go party tonight! Beer's on me"—but enough that I have smokes and that. I phone once in a while to see if he's got anything, but he got his truck stolen with all his tools so now he can't even work!

I don't have a phone so it's kind of a Catch-22. You're looking for work but they have no way of getting hold of you. Well, you could keep phoning them, but you haven't got the money to use a pay phone. Some free phones are only open from ten in the morning till five at night, and they've got a waiting list. So when you do get in on a place they say, "Well, could you come in and drop off a resume?" Well, that's fine, but then you have to pay for the bus fare and they've upped that. So that's four bucks a day just going from here to there.

I don't want a lot of money, just enough that the bills are paid so that when I lay down I don't have to worry about the phone ringing and it's a bill collector.

My perfect future? My perfect future, to be happy and healthy. Just to be happy and healthy, to have a job, and I'd like to have a house. I really want to mow a lawn and plant a garden. I'd like to have, not a big house, just a little house somewhere near water. And I want a dog.

3 months later ...

I take a lot of Tylenol 3s, codeine. I hate to say it; it's embarrassing for me. I was addicted.

I tried to quit and then that's when I found that the pain was so unbearable. I tried a couple of times; I just didn't want to have them control my life. Taking the painkillers didn't work; I mean you'd need more and more and more and more.

With Tylenol 3s, it's not like there was a high; it was just a painkiller. It's kind of a trick thing. These other drugs I've tried were in a social environment, whereas this was painkillers, it was prescribed by doctors. I've been taking them since 1993. Long time! Some days my stomach would be just burned from the painkillers. They caused stress, sometimes sleepless nights. I still struggle through that.

Was I on the methadone program the last time we talked?

I'm on meth now, from the painkillers. I've been on it down here for three months. When you hear about people being on methadone you always think of them as the kind of people that were doing needles and all that. I mean that was my impression.

I'm ignorant.

I take thirty-two milligrams a day, but I'm going down. I started noticing that if you don't get your methadone you feel really sick. Have you gotten any hot flashes? That's what it feels like, but it goes for hours, it's constant, it's not like it just shows up and then goes away. I'm not worried about getting addicted to methadone because I'm working down. The program was designed to get you off one substance, like to be on one substance and to work your way down. That's the way that the program was designed. I'm weaning myself off.

I feel lucky now. In the last six months I've seen a lot, a lot to make me be thankful.

I really didn't have it that bad. I hear some stories that I can't fathom!

I'm relating to the Downtown Eastside now, I'm starting to see they're real people! Everyone's got a story, some of them horrific. There's people I look at today and I just wonder how they can even smile. There are a lot of people down here trying to help, but it's a challenging battle. People need compassion. But from where? Nowadays everybody's so busy.

I've been to so many memorials.

My life is in this community now. I have some short-term goals that I'm going to work towards. I want to get work counselling or doing something downtown here, working with people.

One year, eight months later ...

I slipped on the methadone program. My pain came back.

While I was on the program I noticed that people who have an injury and take meth are treated differently. People judge you whether the pain is real or valid and they disregard your need for pain medication. That's what happened to me. I was injured and they wouldn't even give me a Tylenol because I was on methadone. So I did heroin for a little bit and it eased the pain temporarily, but it was expensive, and I slipped back into that vicious circle. As of November 2003, I'm back on the methadone, weaning myself off again.

I'm trying to find a painkiller that isn't addictive.

In November 2003, Pawz wrote the following paragraph to conclude her story.

Moving to B.C. was the best thing I could have done for myself.
Why? You ask.
A place away from place where I had time and peace of mind to regain the self within.
Soul searching.
A realization of life's shortcomings and justice to be served.
Time will tell.

NARRATOR'S AFTERWORD
November 2003

Leslie: Why do you want to make your story public?

Pawz: If my story affects anybody starting over anywhere in the world, they may get a different perspective on how they want to do it. I had to go into a transition house and totally start over again with employment, housing, relocating. I'd say to people, "Rethink starting over." Hopefully, the people who have to start over can have some sort of insight if they end up coming to the Downtown Eastside. They'll have some kind of insight into what could, but hopefully will not, happen to them. If I knew then what I know now—I would have been on guard. There's a lot of things that are overlooked when you first come down here, and you can be easily deceived, conned, scammed. If you do come to Vancouver, don't stay in the Downtown Eastside. Once you get down here it's hard to walk away from it. This is one of the reasons for publishing my story in this book.

And if I can give just a little bit of insight that might lead to government funding for safe houses and shelters ...

This story is a reminder of what the real world is. It's not just your little job and your home and your family; there's a lot more to the world.

Getting my story out there will give people some insight into that.

Who do you want to read this?

I want someone with curiosity to read this, hopefully somebody who's never been through this and never will go through it. But if they do have to, then maybe they will remember that I survived so they can, too ... I got introduced to pain medication after an accident. When I came here, I was introduced to something that was "pain enlightening" and I ended up getting caught in it.

I could never foresee any of this happening to me.

Speaking as someone who's now lived both sides of the coin—rich and poor, wearing both shoes—you are treated so differently when you have no money. God forbid you ever have to walk on the other side.

A lot of people, when they get down here, they start thinking suicide. I wouldn't cop out that easily. I thought about it a couple of times, but I knew I was better off to fight than to give in. I think I've withstood the test of time (*laughing*).

Being here has made me stronger, and it's made me more in touch with myself, more aware of other people and their plight. I'm not the only one in this position, and I won't sit in a corner going, "Poor me, this shit happened to me." Down here a lot of crap happens to a lot of people, it's not just me.

If this story applies to you, don't lose hope.

Two

LAURIE

EDITORS' INTRODUCTION

In the summer of 2003, a notice appeared on the bulletin boards and doorways of agencies throughout the Downtown Eastside. The headline read: "ALERT—Irreversible Brain Damage Possibly Linked with Certain Drug Use Practices." Toxic leukoencephalopathy[3] is associated with smoking heroin or, "chasing the dragon." In December 2003, 17 heroin smokers from rural and urban communities in British Columbia were affected. Their symptoms included confusion, loss of control over muscles and extreme weakness. In seven cases death occurred. When public health officials examined the substances cut with street heroin and the method by which it is inhaled, they were unable to explain the cause of the condition. For those who use illicit drugs, knowledge about drug purity, and using practices, as well as street ethics and drug-associated illnesses are important elements of harm reduction. "Hiding in Plain Sight" tells of Laurie's struggle to maintain her sense of well being within the shifting terrain of the drug economy. She shares information essential to those who manage their own daily access to, use of, and sometimes, sale of drugs.

By offering observations on the hyper visibility of drug-using residents in the Downtown Eastside, "Hiding in Plain Sight" confronts what we see and what is veiled; what we hide and what we reveal. Laurie openly challenges stereotypes projected upon the people in her neighbourhood by discussing how privilege and wealth serve to conceal, and thus protect, those in other neighbourhoods from stigmas associated with illness and illegal activities.

Stereotypes convey static images, portraying little about diverse histories, diverging political opinions, or acts of resistance and hope. Through the course of ten interviews, Laurie offered critical perspectives on colonialism, social spending, public safety, and health. She rejects ideas of victimhood; instead, she celebrates the skills that enable her to survive.

---

3. Toxic leukoencephalopathy occurs when a toxin alters the white matter of the brain.

Hiding in Plain Sight

Edited from interviews conducted May 2001–February 2003
Interviewer: Leslie A. Robertson

I grew up with friends who were rich; I grew up with friends who were poor. I had the best of both worlds, if you think about it. I had the best of both worlds, having foster and birth parents there—as opposed to just having one set of parents.

I think I had it pretty well in both worlds.

I was born in Regina; I'm Cree. My band is ———; that's my great-great-grandfather's last name, so that's my family reserve. When I found out that name I was actually pretty proud of it. I found out when I was about twenty-five or twenty-six.

But I'm pretty proud of my dad's side of the family, too, even though in Saskatchewan we've got a really bad rep. I taught myself not to judge anybody because I don't like to be judged myself.

I come from a family of seven brothers and two sisters—all are halves. I'm the only one of my daddy's children. I don't remember us doing anything as a family. When I was younger my mom used to say I acted and looked like my dad. Mom wouldn't let us see him. It's weird calling him Dad. I look like my mom.

I grew up in Saskatoon. My foster parents basically took me because I'm half white. I would never step foot on a reserve, I was scared! My foster parent told me if I was bad the Natives were going to come and steal me and never see me again. In Saskatoon I didn't even associate with Natives (*laughing*). I was terrified.

So it's all what you're taught, and then sooner or later you start thinking for yourself and you don't know your ying from your yang.

I don't know. I still feel like I'm on my own. It feels that way.

It's a weird relationship between me and my birth mom. She did a lot of crap to me when I was a kid. I remember we lived in this house, and when she got drunk—that was the worst part, when she drank. She drank a lot. My foster mom was awesome, she read my other mom so good, "Well, your mom's going to get drunk. She's going to give you money, she's going to go to the bar." That was exactly what my mom would do. Every visit; I went for visits only.

"If she does that, just phone us and we'll come and get you."

With not using [drugs], I remember more things than I ever have before. My mother grew up in a foster home too. I remember sitting at the top of the stairs and listening to her talk about how they would beat her. Now I can understand why that went on in our house.

There were a lot of weird people who used to come to my house when I lived on the farm with my foster mom. In my city there was a bunch of kids that went missing. The guy was fixing our house—the guy who was killing these kids—he used to sit in our kitchen. My foster parent just lost it, "He was sitting right in our living room!"

I was a teenager. Where they found the bodies is now an industrial area. That's one thing I don't like about those buildings—ghosts. I believe in ghosts big time.

You never know if it's a good ghost or a bad ghost.

I met a ghost—my foster dad. He was dead five years before I got there, but I still call him my foster dad. I met him in the bushes on the farm. There was a bunch of us kids playing in the yard, no older than fifteen. Now, to get ten, eleven kids to stop at one time and look at one spot—you know, it's pretty bizarre. I saw that guy standing there and everybody got scared. I guess just the thought of somebody standing there scared us. But when I went in the house I saw his picture on the wall. I go, "That's the guy that was standing there staring at us." My foster mother's jaw dropped.

At night-time, you could hear people walk around the house on the farm. I swear to God they were cooking something like bacon. I could smell it, but there's nobody in the kitchen, there's no lights on—nothing—and I'm the only one up in the house ...

I used to be scared of ghosts but my foster parent said to me, "If you're not bad then you have nothing to fear." I thought about that because later on I found out the room that she was sleeping in—that I would sleep in with her—was where they kept all the coffins. Well, her mom died and they kept a coffin in that room. Her son died. Her husband. Her grandchild died. All the coffins, they had them in that one room. Even in my dreams I will not go in these rooms. When I go back to places in my dreams, I will not go to these places.

My foster mom passed away when I turned sixteen. Back then legal age was sixteen, and I was in the midst of moving back in when she passed, she died. My finger used to be straight, but after my foster parent died—her finger used to be crooked—one month after she died, my finger went like that too.

So there's a little bit of my foster parent with me yet.

During my party days in Saskatoon I was living with this other girl and two men. We rented a house for 800 bucks, the whole house. Well, actually, she owned it; everyone paid 200 bucks apiece.

Oh, Christ, I used to drink a lot! I'd break bones. I broke my hand—the bone popped out the end—and I had both my knees broken. But the thing is, I didn't feel it because I was drinking. Acid was my big kick. And mushrooms, when I used to drink a lot, I used to get mushrooms. Tequila Night, I'd go to the bar with forty bucks and twenty-eight grams of mushrooms. I'd come away the next day with a dollar and half a gram (*laughing*) and hung over galore! We were drinking margaritas, paralyzers—oh, Christ! We had our own table, but it got to the point where we couldn't even go to the bar just for a social drink without everybody thinking we were having a party. I came home one night; there was over 200 people at our house. Took me about forty-five minutes to get from the sidewalk to my bathroom (*laughing*).

I moved away from Saskatchewan just to get away from my family.

I always lived in their shadow because of my last name. Cops don't like us. They don't like us because a lot of us got in trouble. Some people tend to be friends with us just because of our last name. It's a bad name (*laughing*), it's well known on the streets.

I woke up one day and I had these two tattoos. Believe it or not, my arm used to be a lot fatter because I used to weigh over 300 pounds. My family said I always forgot who I was (*laughing*). One time I passed out and I woke up four days later. My cousins tattooed my name on my arm while I was sleeping. I guess it's just like having a marking, you know what I mean? Like it's on the map. I belong to a line that may die off, but the thing is, that name will be there forever. So, that's pretty cool! I'm quite proud of both families.

I remember the first time I ever got into trouble. I was eighteen.

I took the rap for my friend because she just got out of jail and I didn't want her going back. She punched somebody out, and I said, "Well, I did it." I got her off. I had no problem with that. When I was in jail, the guard comes by, "Typical [of your family], getting into trouble!" Jail in Saskatchewan was really different from jail out here. The guards are harsher out there. If you got caught holding another girl's hand you got charged. If you accidentally took one of the guard's pens, you got charged an extra two weeks, something like that. Just sticky little rules. They're more strict and they don't have half the shit they have out in these B.C. jails.

It was weird in Saskatchewan because a lot of the guards and a lot of the new RCMP people were people I went to school with. [An old friend] was going in to be a city police officer, and we used to still have coffee all the time. She took me out for lunch one day and she said, "Well, I have something to tell you."

I went, "What?"

"Well, I'm going in to be a police officer."

I said, "Whatever makes you happy. I'll still be your friend. I don't care. You're doing your thing, I'll do my thing."

She maintained the same attitude all the way through, which is cool.

I left Saskatchewan actually a couple of days before I was supposed to get married. Oh, I jilted him good! I was working in a bakery in the morning and a bar at night. He worked construction, and every time he got paid he always gave me some money (laughing). I gave him back most of his money before I left, gave it to his mom. Then I hopped a bus. "I'm outta here!"

I went to Alberta. I stayed there for a good five or six years.

About a year after I moved there I hooked up with this one girl right off the hop (laughing). I hung around with her sister for about a year before I met her. I met her on Friday the 13th; it was a full moon, I remember ... It was a long time ago.

I was in awe, and actually that was the first woman I was ever with. She was exactly one year, one month, and one day younger than me. Everybody thought I would end up dead because she was on remand for murder, but she beat the charges and I ended up with her (laughing). That lasted a whole five years.

The freakiest thing about this was, when I moved to Alberta, I didn't tell my mom nothing—like where I moved or anything. Then, about a month later, something like that, my mom moved into the house right across from where I lived. So then we argued a lot and I left everything I had. I left my partner, everything I had. I think I sort of knew I was leaving. I took my partner out the night before, spent major cash on her, and I said,

"Well, see you tomorrow." I left the next day, came out to Vancouver for a year. I hooked up with my cousin out here and got really into the dope big time, a lot of coke.

Then I went back to Saskatchewan for a year, and I turned into a little alcoholic again. Coke in Saskatchewan is really hard to get. Well, I basically didn't look for it (laughing). Tweaking around in a small town! God! I just substituted it with drinking.

I lived in a little town and got a job with this guy I used to go to school with. So I was working with him out in this teeny little town, 200 Ukrainians, one little Native (laughing). It was actually pretty good; we had a lot of fun, running a [business] together.

I had the cheekiest little baby cat you could find around. I found this little white kitten, and I made a little harness for it to walk beside me. What did I name that cat? I can't remember. It was just a baby. I said, "Okay, I'm going to go for a walk." I put on the harness, it didn't like it and I said, "All right, then you stick right beside me then," like this cat understood me. So we walked around downtown and this little cat is just walking beside me, tail right up in the air. Cheeky little bugger!

I really liked it out there.

I guess Saskatchewan's good if you want to retire but I got the urge to come back out to Vancouver, so I left. (Sighing) It was humdrum. I just got really antsy again, so I said, "Well, time to go."

I stopped in Alberta for about a month or so and came back out here. I've been here since around 1990. I was in my twenties, but I was still very irresponsible (laughing). I came out here, didn't tell anybody I was leaving or nothing. I didn't tell my mom where I was coming, but she found me. When I got here thirteen years ago, I hit the 100 block, and that's where I stayed for a good five or six years! I made my money there; I made a lot of friends. A lot of times things weren't as bad as people seem to think they are.

When I first came here, no one would help me, wouldn't even give me directions! No whites and no Natives helped me, the Spanish people did. I looked Latino; a lot of people thought I was Latino. I got nabbed by immigration, too, four times already. "Show us your papers or we'll deport you!"

Things used to be really busy on that 100 block—I mean really, really busy. It was like going into a mall on Thursday night when it's just packed and they have a big sale. That's what that street used to be like; all the stores were there, all the dealers.

So basically, the 100 block was my whole life for five years. Five frigging years! I didn't think life existed past this block. I lived here, did not leave it. I thought people fell off the face of the earth when they left the 100 block. When I did decide finally to leave, it's like I walked into an imaginary wall, like I took a step and I had something pressed up against my face. It was as if I couldn't go past this boundary.

It was about not knowing what's beyond that. The not knowing is the scary part, because everybody on the block here knew me. It was like being a little kid because you spend all this time with your parents and finally, when you first go, take that first step, it's scary, really scary—you wonder if there's going to be anybody to catch you when you fall. Eventually I went to the Portland because that's where my friend lived.

Back then I was fixing in the alleys. I'd go one more block, but that one more block was really scary. I could hide on the 100 block so damned good; people wouldn't find me. Hiding in plain sight, in plain view, man! You're looking at me but you're not looking at *me*, you're not seeing *me*. Everybody does that. They don't want you to see them. They don't want you to see the real person, so they're hiding, hiding in plain view. You build up these walls that you don't think anybody can see beyond, you don't *want* anybody to see beyond that.

Drugs do that.

We're here but you can't see us; you can't see the real us.

When I started here, I was sitting with a lady who had been on the street for forty years. I'd only been down here for about six months. She goes, "You're just a baby." I took it as an insult, but after a while I thought about it, yeah I am.

I sit and watch people. For the first five years I was down here, I stuck to myself, I watched everybody. You get to see every different type of person there is and what they're like. I even met a guy down here who used to play professional [sport], and he goes, "Blah blah." He was trying to get a front by using his name because, at one time, he was a big player. Well, I said, "If you're so big, why don't you just go to the bank instead of asking someone you don't know down here for a front." (*Laughing*)

I've met all different types of people down here.

I've met doctors, I've met lawyers, I've met a few nurses. We've got a lot more problems down here than any other area, but the thing is, we don't hide it. We don't hide it, not like the West End people do. There's doctors there, but the thing is, they're closet cases. How many people are doing operations high on drugs? How many people are flying our planes like that? And when they lose everything, they either commit suicide or end up in the loony bin. They have an image to hold. An image.

Drug addicts have an image, too. Yeah, we do have an image. Even down here we've got low-class, middle-class, and high-class; you have the dope and you're up there. But what we don't have is people rallying around us. Everybody says they're going to save you. They can't save you.

It's like when Gordon Campbell[4] said, "I'm just a social drinker." If I ever get busted again I'm going to say, "I'm just a social addict." But people rallied around him. I didn't hear anything about him having to go do day treatment. What's going to stop him next time? Some people hide it better and some people can still function, functioning addicts and functioning alcoholics. You know what? These people have had more shit than you ever had and yet they're still here! And a lot of people are here by choice.

The first five years I was here, I didn't associate with anybody. I lived in the same building as my partner and we never even knew each other. I lived in one hotel for nine months. That was before they came in with this ten-dollar guest fee, four or five years ago. Back then it was pretty disgusting; don't leave your dope on the table unless you want your cockroaches to do a chicken!

I felt safe there because I had a lot of people protecting me.

You know, if the walls could talk in these hotels they would have stories to tell you, man!

I heard a freaky story about one hotel. During the thirties, I guess, they had a bunch of squatters in there. The cops came in and three people jumped out the window. I know I've heard this window fly open in there at about two o'clock; this window opens automatically down the hall. If these walls could talk!

There was a dead body in another hotel for four months, and the owner told us we wouldn't even know what a dead body smelt like. When you went past the floor you could smell it; there was a dead body wrapped in a rug. When I walked into one hotel for the first time, it was like those old movies. You're walking up the stairs and everybody's doing their fix and

4. The premier of British Columbia was charged with drunk driving while vacationing in Hawaii during the Christmas season in 2002. Other than some adverse publicity, personal embarrassment, and a relatively small fine, the premier suffered little for his transgression.

their hoots. On one floor, when I was there, there was a bunch of cocaine users. Then we had the heroin users on another floor. Cocaine addicts don't like heroin addicts; heroin addicts don't like cocaine; and heroin and cocaine users hate drunks!

I don't like heroin, although I used to smoke it. I wish crack was like heroin—that I could take it or leave it. Some people can do one or two papers and still sit there. I do one or two papers and I'm lying there, cold turkey. I used to smoke it or snort it; a couple of times I fixed it, and I died. I really turned blue. The first time, my friend tasted the dope and she told me, "This is up." As soon as I got it in me, I sat down and I went, "This is not up." The next thing I know, I wake up, I've got this thing rammed down my throat.

I remember to this day my very first hit of coke.

Everyone wants to get that ultimate high again.

I could put $500 worth of dope in my body, by myself, in half a day. I never saw past my rig. I used to call my fix in the morning my breakfast. There was lots and lots and lots and lots of dope! Everybody had to share their drugs then, at least everybody I hung around with.

I used to do acid and everything else; I used to make a lot of money off that, too. All I did was work, work, work, work, work, dope, work, dope, sleep, work, dope, dope, sleep. If anybody checked all the money I made selling drugs, I'd give Donald Trump a good run for his money. And I had people trusting me, like nine out of ten packers or steers down here; everybody had their preference.

One summer, it seemed like every steer was ripping off their regular customers and I was getting them. When I first started up, I used to be able to stand and talk to everyone. Everybody used to come to me, which was great, but then it got to be a bother. I figured I was getting too big, so I shut everything down.

The problem—number one—is watching your back.

People get jealous. People can't be happy if you're happy. I made so much money; I make a joke about it. You know the six-million-dollar man? I've got so much dope in me, wring me out and you'll probably get high!

The first trafficking charge I got was not here in B.C.

My lawyer at that time said, "Well, the prosecutor is asking for two years and up and the best I can do for you is two years less a day."

I said, "Well, the best I can do for you is fire you!" So I fired him. I represented myself and got four months.

I was caught with 800 hits of acid and about twelve ounces of pot.

The judge said, "How do you plead for possession with the purpose of trafficking LSD?"

I said, "Well, your honour, I could fill up this whole court room. There'd probably be a line-up going down the street of people who could tell you that I take twenty just to get me off. So this is just personal."

I got put down for simple possession, and then he goes, "Well, how do you plead to possession of marijuana?"

I said, "Well, your honour, you got me there!" I didn't know what to say. So he gave me another two months for that one.

I got probation the first time I got caught out here. The judge looked at me, and he goes, "Well, what have you been doing for ten years?"

I say, "Well, your honour, not getting caught!" Because I hadn't been in trouble for more than ten years, and they were just in awe! He goes, "We'll give you probation this time."

My probation officer liked me. I hit him up for bus tickets all the time, every week, and I only had to see him once a month. I had one appointment or another to go to. That's my third trafficking offence.

I had a no-go zone the last time I got caught. I was not supposed to be in the 100 block, and where do I get caught? I knew as soon as they saw me and our eyes met—I knew. Busted! I knew the police officers; they knew me. I got forty-five days for trafficking crack. Actually, I would have got longer, but the cops that busted me went and talked to the judge because of all the community service that I was doing. I had a package that I couldn't get out of my sleeve fast enough. I had just made four rocks, I was ready to smoke two in a pipe, and I figured, "Oh, Christ, they're going to search me!" So I swallowed the rock. I stayed in jail all weekend; they didn't even search me! Oh, I choked. I slept the entire time; they gave me Valium to sleep. I was in my glory sitting in that jail. It was like a little house, if you think about it, 'cause they have bunk beds in them and they've got a little place where you can eat your meals and they've got a toilet. I says, "Here's my bedroom, that's my living room down there, my kitchen and my toilet!" And then when they tried to put a girl in the same cell as me I kept trying to close the door (laughing). "I don't want her in here."

Sometimes it's hard. I feel like I'm leading a double life, like Clark Kent and then Superman the next minute (laughing). That's what I get for working down here for over ten years! People see you walking down the street, "You got anything? You got anything?"

"Leave me alone, I just woke up!"

To keep your customers, you do have to be good. Like, I was told I would make a very good salesperson (*laughing*). I tell people the truth. They'll go, "Well, have you tried the powder?" I'll tell them yes, or no if it's not good, then you take it from there.

It's all chemical stuff now. Even when you do a whack of coke, you're not getting high off the coke; you're getting high off the cut. People don't realize that. It's the cut you're getting high off. Everybody cuts it with different shit. One time they were cutting it with PCP. We had people jumping out of buildings! Christ. They can cut anything with crack, and the thing is, it goes in your lungs and you're screwed! One guy throws a little heroin into his coke. It's very smart. People are buying your dope; they may buy someone else's but they're not going to get high so they come back to you. It's just the business.

The addicts had, like, a code of ethics, but now, since the rock came, that went out the door. More violence, people get more withdrawn. Once you get that rock people will argue over two bucks or fifty cents. The more I get into it, the more I find I don't care, my morals go right out the door. I find I'm more aggressive and I don't like it. It's just getting that next thing, like it's only a five or ten-minute rush and then you're looking for that again.

That stuff is vicious. I did everything for it! I'd steal for it. Lie. "No, no no. I can control this. I can control it." Yeah, yeah.

> You slowly crept into my life
> Before I knew it
> I couldn't keep away from you
> You were there, pretending to comfort my pain and sorrow
> You were the only one that mattered to me
> I thought you were giving me life
> I did not realize
> You were sucking life out of me, inch by inch
> I stayed and defended you with all my friends
> Not listening to them telling me that you are destroying my life
> Making me blind even to myself
> You got me lying to my friends and family
> And then when I decided to leave you
> You made me hurt
> Knowing that I'd come running back
> Because no one or no thing has touched me like you did
> When I leave you, I learn new things
> But now and then you creep into my mind

Making me want and need you
Those secret rendezvous are killing me
You hate the fact that our meetings are becoming fewer and fewer
And that you no longer have that strong a hold on me—no longer
But even through our twenty-five-year relationship
You have taught me at least
one thing without
knowing it:
respect for life and people—
And that we can never be again.

I sit down sometimes, and I write words down the way it comes to my head, the way it just comes the first round. What I want to say comes out without sounding too mushy. That poem—you know how they say someone's not good for you? Well, the dope was that, but you don't see it until it's too late. It's already run you into the ground so harshly. Having the drug as your lover, you know what? It can be your first love and it can be your last love, it can be the one that kills you. It's there to bring you peace of mind, which you want at the moment, and you don't have to deal with anybody. Then it becomes the main focus of your life. It gets to the point where it's like a child that demands your attention all the time. The thing is, you're so used to giving into it that you do it, without even thinking, you do it. I guess I'll always feel the effects of it.

Addiction is something ... to get away.

I hid in it so very good. It got to the point I didn't even know if I was doing it for the right things anymore. It just became a part of me. Well, my mom died; so there's no real reason to—you know. My daughter died, so—you know. It's just because a lot of things have happened in your life. It builds up, but you don't look at it that way. You don't have to deal with it. Here I am in my own little world with my trusty companion—my addiction, knowing we're invincible—you can't break us. That *is* a pact, if you think about it; it's like first love or your best friend. But both of them could kill you or bring you through so much grief. You blame it on everybody but the thing that is doing it to you.

When I used to fix in the back alley a lot, my daughters would come looking for me there. I was just choked, but they were persistent; they kept looking for me. The alleys used to be packed with people, just like the street. Here, you would find everybody; they'd be fixing up and down there. We've had everybody doing everything down here. It's just like walking into nightmares.

It has changed so drastically in the last year or so. It's the crack. Before, people used to fix in the back alleys, not on the street. The tour vans come by and just stop right there, and the next thing you know, they're taking pictures of everybody doing stuff in the back alley. So a few addicts got pissed off. That problem went on for five or six years. It was like, "Hey, you're making money off us and we're not getting anything." Everyone else seems to be getting rich! And they say we've got everything down here? No, we don't. Money's supposed to go to make things better here, it doesn't. That's really pissing me off.

They never had an understanding of the addicts.

Now, they're getting younger and younger down here. Kids! Fourteen-year-olds on school days sucking away at a pipe! When kids come down here they play kids' rules, kids' games. But when you come down here you're playing adult games. And you know what? There's no rules!

See, that's what they have to understand.

There was a twelve-year-old smoking crack down here. There was a mother carrying her kid from back alley to back alley getting high. It pisses me off, but I have no right, no place to say anything yet.

I can't say, "Well look at me."

"Well, you used to use!"

Well, okay, but I work from a lot of mistakes I've made. One mistake actually cost me my daughter, and I don't want *them* to go that far. My daughter thought it was so cool, what I was doing out here; but it's not cool! It was plain stupidity, and now I try to make the best of what I've got left.

I was careless out there. For a three-second mistake, I'm paying for the rest of my life. One girl, we didn't know that she was HIV positive. None of us did; there was eight of us. Out of eight, one or two of us are still alive. The other ones couldn't handle it when they found out. When I found out, my friends were gone. They overdosed. They just couldn't handle it or they gave up. That was over ten years ago.

I started straightening out and I started to get sick a lot, catch colds really easy. I thought, "Oh, if this is being straight, I don't want any part of it because I'm sick more often." I think, when you're using all the time, you really don't pay attention to it. When you're using, you just think you're dope sick. That's the way I looked at it.

When I found out I was HIV positive, I started taking a look at my health. I said, "Okay, maybe we should cut this out, cut this out, cut this out." And then I was getting sick, I was catching colds, everything. I was too high; too stoned to know that maybe I had a cold. But now I'm trying to live life a little bit different because I want it a little bit more.

Some days, I just don't feel like getting out of bed. You get frustrated because every time you get sick you go and see a doctor; every time you feel like crap you go and see the doctor, every time something pops up on your body you go and see the doctor. Once you start taking the meds, you're constantly—like every day you have something to do with a doctor. It gets pretty monotonous. It's tiring. The last couple of weeks I take my DDI and I take my other pills when I eat. And that's only once a day; before I was twice a day. Big ass pills! Aggh, it's tiring. It's not easy to do every day!

Some days I just don't feel like getting out of bed.

I go every day for meds. They won't give me carries because I let them sit there. I get too preoccupied, then I forget where I put them. Life, just everything day to day ... it gets tiring taking them every day. Once a week I see a doctor at a downtown clinic. They check my weight out. I've lost a lot of weight. I say, "Yeah, I've lost a lot of weight. That's why I'm down here, trying to find it." (*Laughing*) I've reached a point in my lifestyle right now, which is slowly improving. It's a long, long haul, but I'm going to see this one through.

I keep thanking somebody; thank you for letting me learn this much.

At least let me do half of what I want to get done.

But there's still a lot more that I need to get done.

I think the hardest part was actually telling my mom that I'm positive. I got my friend to tell her. I remember that because I just finished doing a whack in the back alley and I saw my friend, who was a really good friend of my mom's. I said, "Can you tell her?" I felt like a big thing had been lifted from my shoulders; at the same time I turned around and said, "I'm going to go back into the alley."

Then I had to deal with my mom. My mom blamed herself for my getting HIV. "If I didn't give you the money, if I didn't do this, if I didn't do that ... "

I told her, "Well, Mom, I would have got the money anyway, and you can't blame yourself. I need your support, not your sympathy. I can get sympathy out there, no problem. I'm not asking you for support with money, I'm just asking to help me make it through."

When I found out, I wouldn't even go near people. When I still did my dope I wouldn't let people go near me. A lot of people found out downtown, all in one shot, when this girl wanted to fight me. I heard you can't fight when you're positive. If my blood gets mixed up with hers I will be held accountable for it. There was about fifty people standing there, saying, "Fight! Fight!"

I said, "I can't fight you." I finally said, "I can't fight you because I'm positive," and a lot of people said, "I will take care of you." It was just weird, it changed things; but there's people out there who do care. Then you get the rotten apples in every batch, they don't care because they think their life is the pits. Most of these people just take time.

There's still a lot of women stuck in a rut, they don't think they can change, and they totally give up when they find out they're positive. They're the mothers, they're the caregivers and it really hits them hard. But if I can show them that it is not over with ... it's only over when I think it's over. It's my choice, if I want to live or die, and right now I choose to live.

I feel bad for my friend. She found out that she's positive. She's young.

I saw her and I go, "What's the matter?"

She goes, "I'm dying!"

I go, "What do you mean you're dying?"

She goes, "I got hep C."

I go, "Baby, you'll live!"

She goes, "And I'm HIV."

I go, "Now get off the pity boat. How long have you known me and how long have you known I've been positive? I'm still here. Now the choice is yours. The choice is yours whether you want to live or die. You're the only one that can make that decision."

She just looked at me.

Some days I think I've made a bad mistake but then, you know what? I'm pretty happy I made the choice [to stay alive]. I try to keep thinking of positive things that I've done in my life.

Being HIV positive you lose a lot of things. You lose your family in most cases. You lose a lot of your self-esteem. A friend from the same reserve, he went back home and they wouldn't even help him. Going home is actually one thing that's been on my mind lately, but after hearing that I totally decided not to. They're scared. Scared of something they don't understand. It's very narrow there yet. Like my aunts, they don't know what I've got. I know that for a fact now because when methadone first started coming out there, probably at the drugstore, my aunts were so happy.

"You can come home! They've got your medicine here!"

I'm thinking, "Well, if only it was only that!" But it's not that. They will not be able to contend with what I will go through once I start getting sicker. And I don't think I could contend with being treated like an invalid by all these people that are my family. I cannot do that. It's their own narrowness. They don't want to take the time until it affects their world, and even when it does affect their world, they want to push it underneath the rug.

You know what? You're going to trip over that rug one day.

They figure you might come and infect them. If the illness originated from the reserve I don't think they'd have any problem with it. But because it's more like a white man's disease they don't want it. I'm not ready to deal with that. I went through enough rejection already in my life; I don't need to open up new doors just to get more. One day I would like to go back. But for them to honestly look at me and say they love me, "everything's okay, we're here," I can never see that happening. My mom had a hard enough time dealing with it. When she got drunk, that's when everything came out, but that's something I coped with because I loved her. They want me to go back so bad but they don't even know what they're setting themselves up for. I don't want to dump that on my kids.

My daughter who passed away was the one who was always gung ho. She went out and read everything about HIV, and she goes, "You know what, Mom? It's not that AIDS that will kill you, it's that cold." That made me feel so good because she was taking the time out. My eldest daughter, I don't think at that time she really wanted to know anything about it, but she started coming around a little bit. She told me that somebody said maybe *she* has HIV. I go, "No you don't, if you did, you'd know it a long time ago." This happened to me because of my carelessness out here. As far as I'm concerned, three seconds; for a three-second mistake, I'm paying for the rest of my life.

I tend not to tell my family what I'm up to because they really don't like my friends. My ex came out here and I had one working girl out at my house visiting. One of my brothers out-and-out told me, "Why do you hang around people like that? We don't associate with these kinds of people."

I'm just sitting there thinking, "Oh, what you don't know!"

They still wonder why I live down here. Everything I need and want is here; I've got my partner, I've got my doctors, I've got my pills.

I like where I am right now.

Sometimes I wonder if coming to Vancouver was the best choice. I can't change anything. I lost my mother out here to cirrhosis of the liver. The last time I saw her, the nurses tried to tell me she wouldn't even know I was there. They had her really doped up, but as soon as I said something and I was in the room, my mom called for me. The night she died, I was baby-sitting my friend's kid, and, during the night-time, I knew she had died. I just woke up and I knew she was gone, but I didn't want to believe it. We got along so perfect before she got sick. I tried taking care of her as much as I could ... but she never made it. I was mad at her for a long time for leaving me. In my old house, just a little while after my mom died, I situated a mirror. It was really weird, because I situated it in such a way that I could see my mom standing there. My girls swore it, too; they thought they saw her standing there. Well, I knew my mom was there. I knew my mom came back looking for me because even the lady who lives there now says my mom comes back there looking for me.

I got TB and pneumonia, and, as weird as it may be, I almost died exactly a year after my mom, but they said I've got too much spunk in me. I was in hospital for about a month. I couldn't eat anything, just basically drank these big pitchers of water they give you.

My middle daughter came to the hospital and she said, "Do you want money? What do you want?"

I said, "Ah, buy what you want," so she bought me eight dollars' worth of junk food (*laughing*). Again, I didn't see the signs. Me and my mom, we had just started getting along, we just thought on the same level and then she passed away. My middle daughter, we just got along perfect and then ...

I remember the last time I saw her. I was doing the last two weeks in BCCW and they were just transferring her over. We spent these two weeks together. The hardest part was closing the door and walking away. I can still see her face when I look back. That was the last time I saw her. When I went to her funeral it didn't look like my baby. I kept staring at her, hoping she'd wake up. It just seems like when we start connecting, something happens ...

My middle daughter, I called her the runt of my litter because she's the feistiest one of the whole bunch. Of all my four kids, they pass me this little kid, tiny little bugger, no hair. My son's hair stood up (*laughing*), he had a lot of hair and it stood up. My eldest daughter's hair stood right up too, she looked like a punk rocker. My youngest daughter's hair was the same. So those three kids, I knew right off the hop, are going to look like each other. My middle daughter was the smallest one of all of them, and I just babied her a lot—really, really babied her. It was just like looking at a little me; we were identical. Something I never want to deal with again is losing a kid. I wasn't prepared to lose my daughter, not that way. I thought she was safe in jail, but even there you're not safe.

I want so much more for my children. With my eldest daughter, you know, I've never told her how I'm so very proud of her because she has not taken my route or Mom's route. She doesn't drink; she doesn't do drugs.

I am so proud of that, and she's sticking to her guns! I'm scared if I make that connection, something's going to happen again ... I still have a tendency not to try to get close to people. I let people, to a certain extent get close to me; but then when I find that they're getting a little too close, I find ways to push them away. When I get all bottled up, I always go back downtown because I'm doing business so I don't have to think about it.

A lot of people have died lately. In a two-year span, I lost my grandfather, a cousin—two of my cousins, in fact. In the last little while there's been a lot of people. I can picture their faces but I can't bring up their names right now. Every time they tear a building down, someone I knew died with it. That makes it sad. I don't go to funerals; if I did I would spend more than half my time at them—I would. I tell people not to think I'm cold-hearted. I think I'd rather remember them as they were, alive as I saw them. Maybe the last time I saw them they had a rig in their arm. It's not a very good memory.

They may have left us ... No, they haven't left us! Every person we meet in our life leaves some kind of impact on us, whether we know it or not. You can go ten years down the line, even from your childhood. You sit there and remember; the whole thing replays. They never leave us. Everybody's left an impact on each one of us, even the ones who play the hard cases down here. You know what? If you pass that wall, they like you because there's a part of them in you.

I think out of all of them, it's been my mom and my daughter's deaths that hit me the hardest ...

Somebody told my mom one time that I overdosed, and I used to joke about death. I used to joke about it big time. I'd say, "Look, swear to God, I see me standing over there."

She says, "Don't you dare say anything like that!"

I was telling this lady about a dream I had about my daughter, my daughter that passed away.

She says, "That means you're going to pass away soon."

I said, "I'm not afraid to"—because I'm not.

Last year I overdosed a second time. I was with someone else who said, "This is the up. This is the down." I did it, I sat down and I go, "Oh, for fuck's sakes." I didn't even get the "sakes" out and I was already out, I was already blue. They cracked a couple of my ribs doing CPR. They lost me three times, so technically I was a goner for forty-five minutes, and I still came back. I swear I saw my mom standing there, sad. That was the last thing I remember—seeing her standing there.

I didn't see no bright light, I can tell you that much!

But when I came back, it felt like a part of me was missing, big time, like I didn't belong anymore. I guess I tried so hard, I just felt like part of me was missing because I'd gone away, a part of me was gone. Non-existence. I didn't feel like I belonged here. I talked a bit with other people, and they felt the same way when they overdosed. So I don't even think about it anymore.

Sometimes I get so sick and tired I hope I don't wake up.

People must have compassion; it's only human. Everybody in this world's got one addiction or another, whether it's smoking, whether it's coffee, whether it's tea. Let's see, if we took coffee away from everybody, we'd find people on the black market selling coffee and we'd find people who couldn't buy it at the price they want. There'd be shit like that. The thing is, down here, there's always an emphasis on the bad things, not the good things people do. The public has to be more aware that not all people are drug addicts, drunks; there are people down here who have been down here for a lot of years, more than me. This is our home. They have to realize that we're having the same problems and we're getting their problems, from their communities, put into ours.

I wish I could find beauty in everything I look at—I can. I taught my girls not to hate, because they don't want to be judged or hated for the way that they look or anything else. You can dislike what people do, but it doesn't make up the whole person. That's the way I look at people.

I figure I wouldn't have made it this far if I hadn't had the agencies helping me out as much as they do. People are very tolerant of me. I went through a massive mood swing here two or three months back. Anything you could have done to help me was not good. I bitched; if I didn't get it my way then there was no way at all. If it wasn't for a few of the agencies down here, like WISH and the Health Van, I definitely would not be here! I have to say also that the two officers that last arrested me, if they hadn't arrested me, I would be dead. I was very lucky I had people here who were so patient with me. I think that's what a lot of people need down here. I find people saying that it's so easy to ask for help, but the thing is, the people you want to ask for help, they're social agencies, and sometimes you're barred for being an addict—that's just stupid.

Of course you're not going to ask for help, and then you're going to give up hope.

I'm sick and tired of thinking about what is sensitive and what is not sensitive. People that work in high places in agencies, if they cannot take a little criticism, why do they have that job? You expect it to be all roses? Sorry. If it was all roses, everybody would be fixing in flower shops! It's not roses, and if they can't take criticism they're in the wrong job. The whole Downtown Eastside is a community of its own. They want to change it, but changes take a long, long time.

The Downtown Eastside is notorious. It's known as the place where you can buy and sell things cheap, you can buy drugs cheap. The cops think they're doing a big thing but it's costing the city over a hundred thousand just to have those two cops outside Carnegie Centre for a year. What the hell is that going to do? Why don't you just hire security instead of taking taxpayers' money and spending it on two cops just to stand there and look pretty? That's wrong. What is also wrong is the Health Board hiring nurses to come down here who can do nothing but maybe bandage up a wound and do referrals. These ladies went to school to become nurses, not to do referrals. A lot of the people never leave the 100 block! They establish a relationship and then all they get is a referral? You've got this person to build up a relationship, and they can't do nothing because their hands are tied. That's got to stop.

It's ethically wrong and it's inhumane.

The population here is going to grow, which is really scary. The agencies need to rebuild. It is a slow process, but WISH, for example; if they hadn't noticed the women going missing nobody would have. Who would they check in with? PACE, PEERS, and WISH all work with working women. If you didn't have these agencies down here, would we know about these missing women?

If they didn't have the HIV clinics down here, would they know there's people down here with HIV?

If they didn't have youth workers down here, would they know there was that many kids here?

If they didn't have women's programs, would they know what's going on with these women? Would they know how many are getting beaten?

Would they know? No!

They say you can't teach old dog new tricks, but I still find myself learning all the time. When I did decide to straighten out, I knew I was going to fall a lot. I know I still will. I've come a long way in the last five years compared to what I used to be like. I didn't know how to deal with a lot of things. I'm still learning. Sometimes I feel like giving up and going downtown. I'm so used to just being by myself and not having anybody to contend with. Me and my mom were close, but we never, we never once sat down—ever—just her and I. She never asked me how I was feeling or anything. We talked, but just ... not about issues I had.

I find that when I'm not using, I remember things. They creep back in, and out of the blue, they'll pop up. I never thought of them for a lot of years ... and then they're there ... Talking about it is actually, it's something I really don't do, I'm just learning how.

I hide a lot of things; I know that. Basically, I've never had to deal with them. I feel somewhat relieved when I talk about it, and then I think, "Well, why am I saying this?" It's scary. It's just that I'm stuck in the world where it's only me and nothing else matters. When you have to start straightening out, you have to deal with issues. You want to go back to your safe zone. Technically, I think addiction's just a safe zone because that's what we grew up with, and if that's what's in our own head, then we'll always think like that. It will always be a safe zone.

"You can't hurt me in my world! You don't exist in my world!"

For Aboriginal people, okay, "You're Native, you're drunk, you're lazy. You'll never amount to anything."

And you know what? You're actually considered the lowest of the low. With white people, society still will help you because of [your] colour. Okay, you're an addict, but that's only one of the problems. They don't think of other things that go with being Native. They have a lot of issues, like always being told you'll never amount to anything, always being told that you're nothing but a dirty Indian or a drunk. People will take advantage of you because of your skin colour—guys, white guys. The things you see on TV don't help you either, and some of them are close to home, it really makes you think. And if your parents are alcoholic, you want to hide the fact that they are. So you hide in your own world, and when you get in that little world the things that really shouldn't be bothering them, they let bother them. I just said, "Okay, I'm Native. It's not going to change just because I do a fix. I'm still going to be a Native."

All the way through, as far as I can remember, as far as I've seen—like, Saskatchewan is a very racial province, very racial. [Natives and whites] have got this big racial thing between them. "You're an Indian; I don't like you! You're a white; I don't like you." But you know what? You get another colour in there, and you see these two combine, and they go against this other, this other race.

I was totally blown away! I saw it when the Spanish came. There was a group who came here and nobody wanted to serve them, nobody wanted to rent to them, so they were more or less getting pushed out of here. I've seen that big time. When you're a kid, especially in the seventies, basically they wanted you to stick with your own kind. There are also different issues because there's so many different nations and Native cultures here.

They've got more agencies that are willing to help the one race than the other ones. The Aboriginal agencies [didn't] really start popping up until a couple, three years ago. Every counsellor that an Aboriginal person had to deal with was white! "Why should I be talking to you? You don't know what it's like being me! You haven't walked in my moccasins, so how can you tell me you know how I feel?" You can't tell a black guy, "Okay, I know what it's like to be a slave," I seriously can't. Or the Japanese people, when they got stuck in those little camps, you can't say you know what they felt like! You can probably try, but you don't know what it's like, and so everything has basically been sent on from generation to generation to generation.

We've got our grandfathers' burdens; each one of us.

If I was to go see a counsellor somewhere in the West End or something like that, the first thing that will probably go through their head will be, "Look at where you live. Haven't you ever thought of changing things?" You know what? Christ, I like where I'm living; it's not a hotel, it's not a rooming situation. But the thing is, I get so bottled up. If somebody was to make an appointment for me with a counsellor, I'm lost for words. I get stumped; I let things build up inside me. I know counsellors and I know good counsellors, but I don't feel comfortable with all of them. Maybe it's like the authority figure. I love them for being there, but, at the same time, I can't help what I feel like.

I know myself too, like, when I disappear downtown ...

We make up these hooks; this is what's going on in our lives.

Down here, I feel like we do have a lot more options than they tend to realize. It's just finding them. Once you get stuck in that rut of working, going for dope, working, going for dope, you're pretty well stuck. That was me, too—working, going to sleep—and it's an easy thing to get caught up in. Then you wake up late and you're hungry. It's your choice to sleep in that late (laughing). That's why I'm trying to get my groceries early. I've always had my cupboards full all the time. When I'm not bingeing, then I'm eating; at least I've got my food there.

Sometimes I go to PWN. Actually, I've been too tired lately to go to their food bank. I was having problems with my worker before, about getting some shoes, because my feet swell up all the time. She was going to give me a hard time about my teeth, and she always said, "No, no, no, no." So I went to PWN. Ever since they talked to the worker, she's never given me a hard time. This way I [got] some Ensure when my teeth got pulled because they all got yanked at the same time. I have to get a blender from them too. You've got what's called a monthly nutritional allowance,[5] which is an extra $225. You've got to meet one of the criteria to get on it— underweight, wasting—I fit in there: massive weight loss, that's me. I don't really even want that right now, not unless I've got a sure plan and I know who will look after the money for me. My fat money!

I backed off on Schedule C for so long because I'm terrible with money as it is. I do not need that, I'm basically thinking about my health. I'm creative. That's why my rent's directly paid right now. I'd like to keep it like that.

You wouldn't believe it down here! Money does help to make it a bit easier, here and there, but it's still such a burden! I don't like to have money on me because I get this pain in my stomach. I used to laugh at people on TV, you know, how badly they need that fix. Well, I feel like that sometimes if I get money in my hands.

I don't care about money. I think it's a curse!

I find money, I find dope, and I find it in plain view! I found a lot of money on the ground one day and I knew something was going to happen to me! Sure enough, two weeks later I was in hospital—TB and pneumonia. It always happens. I hate finding money. It's the root of all evil.

When I owe money, if I see the person, I give it right back to them. They appreciate when I do give it to them at that time because it's when they need it. It's not like I'm avoiding paying them; there's a timing to it. When I do finally pay someone, they say, "Great, just when I needed it the most!" When they think about it, they're happy they didn't hound me for it.

When it comes to money, I keep a record in my head. I can calculate so fast. I'm used to calculating everything because I've been dealing out there. Over a hundred dollars, I can remember all the deals everybody makes. No matter how high or tired I am, that's one thing I never lose track of—my dope and my money.

I used to be notorious for stashing. You have a tendency to stash and to watch everybody's moves.

The first time I was seeing my partner I promised her six welfare-cheque days in a row I'd be up in our room. I never made it. By the time I made it up to the room, I'd already spent about 120 bucks in one walk, just paying people I owe.

I feel like I'm burning her with what's going on with my life ...

5. At the time of this interview, persons on Disability benefits were eligible for a Monthly Nutritional Supplement of $225 per month, as follows: $165 for food, $40 for vitamins and minerals and $20 for bottled water.

When she gets her cheque, we help each other out, which is cool. People ask why I give her some of my money, like what I get at the bank. There's one thing she's taught me—how to share. It's really good to think about someone other than myself. That woman's a major factor in my life. I was so used to being independent, but now I'm so used to having her there. Just being with myself, it's pretty harsh; with another addict, well, I find we blame each other for a lot of things that go wrong. Not really wanting to admit what's wrong, not wanting to really go there and admit it.

Personally, I've never been into treatment programs or recovery programs, but I've had the opportunity to talk to a lot of people about them. The treatment programs have to be longer, a six-week program doesn't cut it. Each person has told me the same thing; at the end of the six-week program they feel abandoned. If they have a longer treatment program and are integrated back into society, knowing they've still got support and a friend there, that will help them to get new housing. Most of these people don't have a place to go. Okay, if your time's up you've got to go. All these people do is make the bed over and ship a new person in there.

Treatment programs have to be longer.

As far as prevention goes, we can go to all these schools and say this, and this is bad. If any reasonable adult uses that tactic, they're stupid. As human beings, we're always curious, and the curiouser ones are the ones that will try drugs.

Show them all the gory pictures and say, "This could be you!" Say, "One time you'll get bad dope." I've got three friends paralyzed from coke; it went right through the spinal cord. "This could happen to you. I'm not saying it will. You will be the lucky one if you make it out."

I've got that monkey off my back, but I don't pressure people because that's one of the worst things you can do.

"Well, if I can do it, you can do it."

"Well, you did it but I'm not you!"

The people that talk like that are the addicts that get on this high horse, but the thing is, that horse will buck now and then, and, when you fall off, where do you go? The people that are cutting us down are the people that are making excuses about why they're using again. They can't say they just couldn't handle it. That's too hard to say.

Everybody's promoting that it's not good to do drugs, okay? But then we've got a safe fixing site from some other country, which, by the way, is having problems with theirs because of crack use. The thing is, you're going to have four or five people doing their dope there who you've never done dope with before. You don't know how they react.

I've had one person say, "Can you hit?"

"Yeah."

She says, "I'll give you one and you can do yourself."

I said, "No problem," I did mine. The next thing I know, her jacket goes over her head and she says, "Don't kill me! Don't kill me! Take my money!" Some people, they get paranoid when they're high. Some won't go to safe injection sites. I'm thinking maybe 40 per cent of people will go. For one thing, a lot of people still like to sit by themselves because they've got their own little thing that they do. Me, I like to clean up, and then I mess it all up again; but other people are different. With cocaine, you do an overdose, you don't come back. Most cocaine overdoses, nobody lives.

People that use rock condemn people that fix but if you blow your lungs, you're toast. They don't seem to see. With this rock down here, you're going to see an increase in TB and lung diseases galore because you don't know what the next person has. You lend your pipe out so you can get the resins. It's going to become a bigger health issue than you've ever seen. With all these cutbacks coming, the population down here is going to grow. Like, it's already started; more kids and more older people and more people with mental health problems. That is the biggest tragedy of it all.

I saw a picture yesterday that I want to buy on welfare day. It's over in Chinatown—a tiger, a great big tiger, hand-painted, forty-five bucks. I think I'll get one for my wall. I figure I'll move into a bigger apartment. I was thinking about this last night because I really do want to move out of the area anyway after I get my teeth done. I want to get my teeth done and get my hair cut.

I think I deserve a break.

I've got a nice place and all, but I don't have the tranquillity or the peace that I want. I want to have a more positive outlook on life than I've ever had before.

I'm 168 pounds now, and quite happy with that. I've got a whole new focus on everything that I want to do. I find myself opening up to a lot more. There's a lot of things that need to be done. I've spent the last few years, if not taking care of somebody, looking after everybody—everybody but me. I gave my last money away to somebody. But now, this is my year. I've volunteered at a lot of places to help keep me sober, but now I'm doing it because I feel the need to. It's helping me to get a better understanding of not only myself but my community.

It's all in the way you approach people.

Leslie: Tell me about the title of your story

Laurie: "Hiding in Plain Sight" is an excellent title.

See, the buses come and go down here, and you see people looking. But they don't see nothing. All they see is the dope. People can hide in plain sight; they can be about this far away from you. Like when they put that new sci-fi movie on TV, *The Invisible Man*—the thing is, these people, they're invisible to society. Everybody looks for one thing and that's the dope. Not the people—the dope. They look at you but they're not looking at you, they're looking through you.

Why do you want to make your story public?

Everybody's been stereotyped to hell!

I'm a person that has HIV—that has hep C and a lot of other things that go with it. I have to learn to deal with it. I want people to know that I come from a broken home, that my mother abused me, but that things don't always have to go that way. Things can change. It took me getting HIV and actually getting right down—sick, to actually take a look and say, "Hey, not everything is bad." Things that happened in the past, you can't let go of, but there is a brighter future out there. There is. Some people look for it forever and some don't. I think I found it. I'm still here and, technically, I should be dead. Each person, I want them to know that they're here for a purpose. They're here for a purpose. Some are learning, some aren't.

I'm mostly getting sick and tired of kids coming down here and thinking it's okay. They come from a broken home—and this and that. I want those kids to know I have a Grade 12 education; I hold two jobs; I have four beautiful kids; I have two beautiful grandchildren. I could have got married but I had a different calling. My calling may not have been the best, but, at the same time, it has taught me so much. Some will make it out of here; some will go down to this pit. Some will crawl out and some won't. I want them to see that it's not as bleak as it looks.

If there's a wall there, you're the ones who can take the stones out one by one. When you've got a big enough space to go through, you go through. It may scare you, but the thing is; you know it's there and then curiosity will grow, everything is new. That's what I want them to know. Life doesn't end just because somebody branded you an addict or an AIDS victim. It's not an ending. That's why I want to publish my story.

What do you think stories like yours can say?

I figure doing my story will be great because people need to understand. You've got six people with six different backgrounds. Some will end up right and some will end up bad. I wouldn't trade any of this for anything. It's learning and accepting; accepting is the biggest, hardest [thing] anyone will do. They can learn all they want, but accepting it, that's the big hurdle. You find out your daughter is a drug addict and a prostitute—get over it! There's a reason why she's doing this and you can't blame yourself. She has things she's got to come to terms with. Nobody can live in the fast lane forever. Sooner or later you're going to run into that roadblock. Some are pretty lucky when they reach that roadblock and some are not.

Your heaven is what you make of it and your hell is what you make of it. I want people to understand. Not everybody's dying here. As bad as they think they are, there's always hope. Everybody, even if they see no hope they see something, and that's a shimmer. They can look and just see a little shimmer.

To every problem there's a solution. To every illness there's a cure and to every bad thing that's gone on in your life, there's always something better at the end.

Did that come from me? (*Laughing*)

Tomorrow, maybe in half an hour, you'll have a housewife leave the family and come into this. First, it's, "I'm going to go mix with the low-lifes." Ten to one, she'll get sick and tired of this life and go home, but there are issues there. Nobody's immune, and it's no defect in anybody. You can only put so much on someone's plate, and one way or another they're going to do their thing. Everybody has a secret they're hiding.

Who do you want to read this?

I fear for the addicts down here but my bigger fear is for the closet addicts; there's still a lot of them. Most of the people that OD down here—and the people that go around bringing them back to life—they're fighting to save somebody who, in most people's minds—not worth it. But say if it happened to a doctor or a lawyer—you want to see what happens when people find out, their families, their colleagues. There's like a little bandwagon behind them. They go to treatment, they do this and they do— but do you ever hear of them ever finding one overdosed? No. They keep their statistics well hidden. Because we're the visible minority—invisible but we're there—they want to keep stats on Aboriginal people, on "addicts," basically. What I'm learning also with the Aboriginal people is, as soon as they find out they're HIV, they're kicked off the reserve.[6] And where else do they have to go where medical help is accessible? Fine, you have HIV. Here [in the Downtown Eastside], you hear a few comments. But you don't get that look because they think you're a junkie. The family issue—like, it's scary to go back. I'll be happy if my family reads this and they understand me more.

Addiction doesn't start at nine and end at five; sorry, it doesn't work that way. You wish it did but it doesn't. It's sad. It can happen to anybody, anybody. If I can get three people reading this who maybe want to check out drugs, maybe they'll see what they're in for. Some days are great—just like at home—but some days are bad.

That's what I would like. Look at this.

---

6. There are hundreds of First Nations reserves in Canada, and generalizations should always be read with caution. While the experience of rejection Laurie discusses is not uncommon to many Aboriginal people diagnosed with HIV/AIDS, there are some First Nations communities that welcome and care for their infected members.

Three

BLACK WIDOW

EDITORS' INTRODUCTION

Black Widow describes herself as a "ward of the government." Orphaned as a teenager and unable to live with strangers in foster care, she began work in the sex economy. In her story, Black Widow describes the Downtown Eastside as a place where, due to conflicting motives and potentially dangerous street scenarios, trust is difficult. She tells of the necessity for some degree of social isolation made manifest in a bold independence, and in the fragility of a support network she has forged with service providers and members of her street family. "Why Me" shows Black Widow's resilience in the face of multiple losses and a history of gendered and racialized violence.

At the time we were editing "Why Me," the Provincial Government of British Columbia was on the eve of enacting legislation to set a two-year limit on social assistance benefits. Thousands of people were expected to receive their last cheque in April 2004, regardless of their need to pay for shelter, food, and other basic requirements. The stated assumption, on the part of policy-makers, was that people would seek and obtain employment and that those unable to do so would fall into a "traditional" safety net provided by family and friends.

For street-involved women that the government deems "employable," the ticking clock presents few safe options, and the change of policy threatens to push them further into often dangerous underground economies. Many women are a long way from home, or estranged from families; they are without the luxury of return. Although Black Widow is not subject to the cuts in social assistance, her story provides some sense of the challenge that lies before those who *will* face the two-year limit.[7]

---

7. In February 2004, the B.C. government added a "last minute" exemption to the 2-year time limit. Previous estimates of the number of people who would be cut off social assistance ranged from 8,000 in Vancouver to 28,000 across the province. Under the exemption, 339 people are expected to lose their benefits. The two-year limit remains on the books and community organizations, advocates, and activists are calling on the government to drop the legislation altogether (*Vancouver Sun*, 7 February, 2004, 1).

Why Me?

Edited from interviews conducted September 2001–March 2002
Interviewer: Leslie A. Robertson

I was born in Edmonton.

I lived there off and on ... off and on ... off and on.

I was mostly raised in Calgary. I lived there for twenty-seven years.

My mom moved a lot when we were little. We moved to Calgary because my grandma owned the house that we lived in and then my dad passed away so I had to go to Edmonton and then Winnipeg, and then my mom passed away. I lived in Winnipeg for a year and a half.

Cold, man! Cold!

My dad died of cancer of the lungs when I was ten and I moved to Edmonton to live with the black side of my family, then I moved back to Calgary.

I started working when I was fifteen, in Calgary.

I was here in Vancouver when I was a girl too, then I went back to Calgary. I was here with somebody for about two years, then I was in Oakalla for about a year.

When I was living in Calgary I met this man in a club there, and he says, "I'm going to kidnap you."

Whatever. Yeah, whatever.

So, he went to Vancouver with his girlfriend and he sent a plane ticket for me to come from Calgary. I sent it back and I said, "I'll come when I'm ready to come! Don't push it!"

I was only, like, fifteen at the time. When I came, I came on my own.

It was a hundred years ago as far as I'm concerned.

I was in Oakalla when I was fifteen.

It was very interesting. It made me grow!

I was in Oakalla because I lied; I got arrested for breach of recognizance. I couldn't be on the block from a certain time to a certain time, and they caught me there and then. Back then they were arresting the American girls on Georgia—we worked on Georgia. I was not from America so they were trying to figure out who I was because they knew all the girls. They sent me up for breach of recognizance, and I was lying about my age, too.

We did a little performance in the gym at Oakalla that was on TV. My mom saw it in Calgary, and she goes, "What is my fifteen-year-old daughter doing in a grown-up jail?"

On the day of my release, they told me I was going home, and I said, "Yeah, I know, it's my release date."

They said, "No. You're going home to Calgary!"

Pissed me off.

I was in there for eight months, and then I had to go into a detention centre. Another year.

My man came to visit me in the Youth Detention Centre there in Edmonton. He's a nice guy. You know what? He's the only guy in twenty-four years, no word of a lie—I never lived with him—and he never hit me once. Not once! He tapped me on the back of the head for getting false nails, but that was it.

He knew my mom and he knows my sister. He knows my family, that's why I'm still with him. He knew my mom was murdered; he knew my mom had a nightclub and stuff like that. He's my friend, my best friend.

My mom had a strip club, she was on ——— Street and I was on ———. My mom was murdered when I was seventeen.

I was put in foster care for—I was going to say about half an hour! (*Laughing*) About half a month. Yeah, not for long!

I don't like being around people I don't know.

No. Not for long.

I've been doing cocaine since I was seventeen, but you know, I've been doing drugs since I was fifteen, just smoking weed and hash. I didn't like hash. I got freaked out. I didn't like that at all. I could only smoke maybe two or three tokes off a joint and that's enough buzz for me.

And it stinks! It makes your clothes stink!

I remember the very first time my boyfriend gave me some coke.

He never even did it with me then. Come to think of it, he doesn't do it with me now! I started doing lines when I was about thirteen. The guy I was seeing had it. We went to a new year's party and he gives his sister something and he says, "Okay, go in the bathroom with my sister and do this."

"Okay, fine."

I snorted some. I didn't know anything about it. I guess I looked old for my age when I was little. I was only allowed to do it on holidays. I worked mostly; I didn't even drink that much.

My boyfriend was murdered in front of me when I was twenty-four.

He went to jail with a guy who was Aryan Nation and who didn't feel that a white guy should be going out with a black girl.

You don't see Aryan Nations too much here, but I'm sure they're around somewhere. There was a little area in Alberta between, I think, Airdrie and Edmonton.

So … he got beat up in front of me. I saw it happen. The paddy wagon pulled up. The policeman said, "We've got a warrant for your arrest." They took me in and they said, "We don't have a warrant, just tell us what happened."

Aggh!

I tried heroin twice in my life, with my stupid friends! I was in my twenties then. I couldn't eat, couldn't sleep. Before I did heroin I did morphine—morphine and cocaine. I used to go with this guy, and that was his drug of choice. We used to do morphine and cocaine, morphine and cocaine. I was in my mid-twenties, he'd get a peeler, and then he'd get the coke. The peelers were eighty dollars; they were grey, orange, and purple. You peel off the codeine. The grey one would cost eighty bucks and the orange one cost sixty bucks. Morphine was more expensive than the cocaine was, so we kept on robbing banks just to pay for his morphine habit!

No guns, no violence, just withdrawal slips—"fraudulent cheques" they call it. I did four and a half years for that.

When I was with that morphine addict, we were fixing every day, every day, every day, every day. I'm allergic to needles, to metal, so I used to shoot, and then I'd get this big rash. You could try anything in the world that you want on me but it didn't work; there was an abscess like that (*gesturing a large bulge on her arm*).

I don't do it anymore.

I was married; I paid for the wedding and I paid for the divorce. The wedding was thirty-five bucks and the divorce was fifty-five bucks (*laughing*).

My ex-husband moved my kids to Vancouver when I was in jail, and I got out of jail and I freaked. I phoned and I said, "Where's my kids?" They told me four hours later, and they gave me the phone number and the address. My friend bought a semi-truck so I came out here in a semi.

I phoned my ex-husband and he said, "How did you get my phone number?"

"Never mind. I've got the address too and I'll be there in a week."

That was nine years ago. Now my kids are fifteen and thirteen.

I came here in '92. I stayed with some people that didn't do drugs. My girlfriend, I stayed with her for a little while. Then I stayed with my ex-husband and my kids and that didn't work out. I had to start all over again in the city.

I was here before, but it's hard in the beginning because everybody wants to tell you what to do and where to go and how to do it when you get there. You have to just kind of work it out on your own. I'm not saying I'm any better or worse than anybody, but I'm trying.

You know, I wasn't really down here long when I was younger, so everything was new to me—more or less. Maybe this drug scene has been here for a long time, I don't know. I just didn't notice it before because I was with somebody and maybe that kept me away from it. Maybe it was there and I didn't know it was there.

When I came back nine years ago, "Okay. I'm lost. Where's Oakalla?" Okay, it's gone.

"Now, where is the Stratford Hotel?" Okay, it's gone.

"Where's the Devonshire?" It's gone too.

They renovated when I was gone (*laughing*)! You know, Cordova wasn't really a gay area and the Black Angus was on Davie and now that's a Denny's. There're a lot of different things that weren't here before. The working girls used to be on Georgia, and I've just found out there's a kiddy stroll.[8] There're a lot of different things that weren't here before; everything's just gone.

I learn something new every day, still to this day.

When I arrived in the Downtown Eastside I was going down the street and I went into the first hotel I came across. I stayed there for a minute and I didn't like it, so I moved to another one and didn't like that (*laughing*).

Crack users used to hang out in the hotel I used to live in and sell it there all the time. Enough was enough was enough!

---

8. A specific area where men seek sexual services from underage girls.

They used to knock on my door and wake me up and sell the shit! There'd be a fight outside my door, there'd be all kinds of bullshit, so I said, "I'm moving! That's it!"

Then my landlord bought another hotel, so I moved there and ever since then I've been cool! I'm paying three seventy-five; it's a nice suite though. It's all right!

They didn't have to tell me at my hotel the other day, but I guess somebody died on the second floor. That's the floor where you can just come and rent a room by the night or the week and then you check out. I guess a couple of nights ago they found a leak in the bar, and they were wondering where the leak was coming from. So they go up to the second floor and they knock-knock (*gesturing*) on every door. The guy died in the shower and had plugged the drain.

I don't know, man, I just came home and they told me.

A month, maybe three weeks ago, they knocked on the door. It was a cop. I was just waking up. I take medication for my legs and sometimes my pills make me forget.

So, I open the door and I go, "Good morning officer!" (*Laughing*)

You know it was like, "What did I do now?"

I guess someone else had died a few doors down from me. I saw the guy around and I didn't really talk to him. Just, you know, just to say hello. I don't really associate with people in the building. So. The guy who died, I guess somebody opened his door at four in the morning and TKO.[9]

Gone.

The cop was asking about it and—who knows what they know about you that you don't know they know, right?—I went, "I don't know when the last time I saw him was. Maybe yesterday. I don't know. I just go home, do my thing, and leave."

I don't bother anybody.

I don't get close to anybody; I just try not to get hurt anymore.

I phone my sister once a month, and my cousin is here, too.

It's just a wall; you build a wall.

I hate Saturdays, so I stay in bed.

Knock, knock; open the door, my friend's trying to tell me his life story. So he comes by, wakes me up, tells me his life story. So-and-so will come by, tell me their life story. "Oh. That's nice—next! (*Laughing*) I've got to go now."

---

9. TKO is a boxing term meaning "technical knock out."

I just don't talk to people about anything, but that's okay. I don't like everybody and I don't dislike everybody. My mother-in-law went in the hospital for a knee replacement, so I've been looking after her. Sad though, she's got seven kids and every time I go there, she's all by herself! Every time I go there, man, there's nobody there! She's bopping around and sleeping on the couch, and I feel so bad, but I take care of her.

Every day I get up and have a shower, brush my teeth, and if I'm going to ———— [Centre], that's where I get my messages. Sometimes I go pick up some money from St. James or my kids phone me. Sometimes I go to ———— [Centre] and watch some of the kids because they come to pick them up at 3:30. Then they've got another half an hour before they close, so most of the moms stay on the phone and that's it. I look after the kids while their mom's on the phone or with a counsellor or whatever. We all leave about four or five. They go their way and I go my way.

After that, I used to go to the bar. People aren't in the bar so much as they used to be. The bar is not really that busy and people are getting really snotty and really persnickety.

Really touchy. Really touchy.

People are tight! Remember in the eighties when people had money? Even in the nineties people had money! People still *do* have money but they're tighter now.

That's history, right?

I really like ———— [Centre]. It's only for women, but it's nice because people talk about things. People, like, they're for real; they talk about things. They have a little newsletter. They did a newsletter on me. I didn't even know they did it (*laughing*). It was cool. I volunteer once a week. They give me two bus tickets and a ten-dollar gift certificate for Safeway. I'm saving them up and I'm giving them to my mother-in-law for Christmas. I just do the dishes, clean the floor and stuff; for three hours, ten bucks— not bad. You have to work for five hours just for a pack of cigarettes when you volunteer somewhere else. That's almost like the joint,[10] because if you work in the joint you have to wait for canteen days, which are Wednesday and Sunday.

But I'm not going back to jail! I'll volunteer!

I like VANDU too, VANDU's cool. The first time you get a job there, it's always an office job. You just putt around this office for four or five hours, answer the phone, whatever you have to do. Then the next week you go on

---

10. Jail.

alley patrol, where you go with the nurse from Victory Park and you do all the alleys all up around Oppenheimer [Park], all the way back to the office. It's about three or four hours. You're picking up the rigs in the alleys and you're giving people new rigs, and if they need medical attention, the nurse is with us so she will patch them up along the way.

It's all right; it's okay.

Tonight I'll work under the tent in front of Carnegie,[11] and that's from eight to twelve—hand out water and some condoms and syringes, band-aids, stuff like that. It's all free. I don't know, I just figure I don't want to be too greedy so I don't take too many shifts.

I haven't really been drinking lately. I go out about nine o'clock and stroll past the bar and look in (*sighing*). I don't know, like, I could go and sit in there and wait for some *foolio* to buy me a drink and be the "ho" that I am, but I've got no desire because I've got no pressure on me. I go in because I've got some girlfriends. They're really bad heroin addicts but they're friends of mine. I don't give a fuck what they do, they're still friends of mine. I always walk in there to make sure they're still alive and they're okay. I haven't drank for two weeks.

As long as I'm broke, I'm happy! I was drinking every day. Every day, man! I was broke but I was drinking every day.

Now, I take my anti-depressant, I take my Ibuprofen,[12] and when I eat I feel tired. I eat and I go home, lie down for a couple of hours, and watch a TV show. I think that I'll watch one show and then I'll go to sleep, but then another show comes on (*laughing*). DOING!

I don't know, maybe when I was drinking lots it made me tireder and I used to sleep more or something.

So, I sit at home and watch all these shows on A & E,[13] like *Simon and Simon*. *Crime Story*'s a good one—that's a doozer, that one! Like so-and-so did something to so-and-so twenty years ago, and now so-and-so is going to throw him over the bridge. You can look at it and you know it's a show, but you can think about it.

I think it's fucked up! You know it's a movie but ...

11. At the time of this interview, the tent sheltered a temporary needle exchange on the sidewalk outside Carnegie Centre, at the corner of Main and Hastings.

12. An anti-inflammatory drug.

13. Arts and Entertainment channel (available on cable TV).

The news is horrible, too, just the pain in the news nowadays, it's—you know, about those kids that just got burnt up?[14] They just found the remains. All the babies were in the house. Where was the wife? They never said nothing about the wife. Just about three months ago there was that woman that drowned all her five babies and then there's another six. What is it? Copycat killers or something? And that Sally Jessie Raphael is a really freaky one. You know, she was doing missing children—all these shows!

They don't really do addicts on TV very much anymore. They're not really doing coconuts or heroin addicts. And they're not really showing working girls either. They're just doing stupid crimes, really stupid crimes.

Like today on *Crime Story* they did a heist in a casino, and they all ended up dead. They got the money back, but they all ended up dead. I don't know, I watch twenty million shows in two days! I fall asleep for half an hour, I shake my head; what did I dream about that for?

I never watched so much TV in my life! Honest to Lord, I don't know what is going on with me.

But I do watch *American Justice*. Maybe, maybe one day I'll find out what happened to my mom. She was murdered and they found her body by the river.

Right now, nobody is bothering me. Nobody, nobody is bothering me.

Nowhere, no how!

I get my phone calls, if I have some regulars or something. They phone me and I go and see them. I have no complaints except that I'm trying to find my kids. I want to talk to my daughter. Last time I saw her was when she graduated. I'd like to see my kids because their birthdays are next month.

But I can't really complain.

I'm not overwhelmed and driving my Mercedes or anything (*laughing*)! Just doing fine, you know?

I'm a woman. It doesn't matter what we want, we get it and then we always want something else. Even if you've got the right man, you know something's missing. There's something wrong with this picture, it's not right.

My boyfriend just got out of jail and it's nice to see him. I was kind of down, sad. Two years is a long time. I don't visit jails anymore. He would phone me or I talk to his mom. I just let him be. He'd phone me collect

---

14. This refers to an incident on Vancouver Island in which a man was charged for killing his six children and burning down their house.

and I'd just pay [the staff], that's the way I did it. I don't like to bug his mom too much, even though I know she's there. He comes out, and then he goes back in, and then I have to give his mom money every month because when he gets out he has to have his money. You know, he got out before and I was still really kind of getting over my car accident and I didn't really have anybody anyway.

I got hit by a drunk driver. That was about three and a half years ago. I was out working at a club. I was going to the bar to meet my friend and TKO; she hit me right on the corner. Gonzo!

Yeah, so seventeen months in Vancouver General Hospital. I have seventeen pins in my leg. It only bothers me when it rains a lot, my toes go like this (*curling her fingers*), I cramp up. But that's okay. You know what's worse is when your kids come to see you and you're half dead. I had to learn how to walk and all that, but I got over it and I'm okay now. I had to go to physio once a week. They used to have to come and take me back to VGH for physio. So eventually I decided to walk.

I don't know if I was diagnosed with hep C when I was in hospital from the car accident or what. I don't remember having it before.

Like I said, I started working when I was fifteen in Calgary. Even my ex-husband would pressure me to go to work. When I was younger my boyfriends would say, "Go to work. Go to work."

I think they were wired, and I was young and I was really naïve. Now I'm not really smarter, I just don't take much shit. I don't work that much anymore because I don't have to. I'm really lazy.

Like, years ago, I remember when I first worked here on Georgia.

I said, "I can't wear a fur coat on Georgia! All it does is rain!"

He'd say, "Put on the fur coat, and go to work."

He doesn't say anything like that to me anymore.

I'm working but I'm not working. No one's telling me what to do so I'm not doing anything (*laughing*)! I'm really relaxed.

Before I slowed down, I made enough money to pay for my habit and clothes; I'm a clothes fanatic. It may not look like it right now, but I am. I've got clothes coming out of my ying yang.

I was going to get a cell phone, but then I thought, "Well, I'll probably lose that like I lose all my umbrellas!" A cell phone—you know, you get busy, just put it down. You don't feel comfortable with a date or something, you put it down and it's gone.

I had one of those days on the ship. These guys, when they don't speak English you don't feel comfortable. You never know what they're saying to each other. You know, you do a couple of jobs on the ship and the rooms are just so tiny. So then, you get two guys in there and you feel (*gesturing containment*). You're trying to be nice and gradually find the stairs to get off.

The corridors go round and round.

That's scary; the last time I was there, it took me half an hour to find my way off the ship (*laughing*).

Sometimes you have to think twice.

I'm not going really far away anymore. No. It's scary. (*Sighing*)

When you think you're cool in the game and all of a sudden you're stuck, you take a second look.

I got stranded a week and a half ago—way, way out by Lougheed. It was a funky date, we had a disagreement, and then he says, "Okay I'll drive you home." We were going down in the parking lot and he let the door slam and I couldn't get back in the car.

Just freaky people.

I had to wait until four o'clock in the morning, so I went to a hotel and I slept in a chair until the buses were running. At least I had money to get home on the bus. But I did hard, good thinking.

I've got to quit taking advantage of things and be cool. I don't like getting high with tricks—I don't—because you know their mind is kind of … they want more, and they want this, and they want it now, and they're really pushy. All guys are.

I don't work with other women because you don't know what they're doing! What if something happens to her and you don't know? It's really, really hard to depend on people, but it would be nice sometimes. It would be nice. If I've known you for years, we can work together; we can be partners. We have a double date—we go on a double date together—okay, fine. You're going to get the same money as I'm getting, we leave at the same time.

If you know somebody that's been across the street forever but you never really talk to them and all of the sudden they say, "You want to get high?"

I go, "Uh, well, maybe later, okay?"

I'm a little sceptical.

I started using drugs with men because you can't trust women.

Everything goes to my stomach now anyway. I don't know what they did when they operated on me, but I just can't have it.

Whatever is in the heroin, it makes you sick. I lost some friends—well, not really friends ... people I know—on the bad heroin that was going around. People are just dropping like flies everywhere, man! People who do that heroin, they seem like they're sick all the time.

Sometimes I smoke crack. Not very often.

If you get some really clean cocaine, you get some really nasty cocaine, too. I phone my friend because I don't know what's in this shit here. I'd like to just give a rock to somebody to take to a scientist to see what the hell's in it. Take one from that corner and one from the middle of the block and then maybe one from another place and take all three of them to the laboratory and see what is in it! You never know.

Sometimes I'll smoke and I'm sick for two days! I've got diarrhoea.

Downtown they ten-dollar you to death on their dumb dope! Of course you can't really get high off it. You can't! I don't know what these people are putting in that stuff! Yuk! It's just so blatant! What are they putting in it to make their faces like that? You know, I don't know if they're picking their faces or what they're doing, but it's just horrible.

Usually I find someone I know, so I know where [the crack] comes from. People make cocaine differently. I know that the coke I get is good and clean when I don't get a headache.

I don't like people talking to me when I'm getting high. It irritates me. My TV, I can handle my TV because I can turn the thing off. I just want to escape from all the bullshit. "Just don't talk to me. Just sit there and shut up, we'll get along fine." (*Laughing*)

Lots of people get high; they go blah, blah, blah, blah, blah, blah. They think I'm joking until I get mad and kick them out. If they don't abide by my law, get out! I don't know, I just think about it; I've put up with pressure all week, now I'm going to have thirty seconds of relief. Then, I think ... am I happy?

No! It's just that the whole world's coming in on you and this is your only tiny escape that you think that you have. It's just your mind telling you nothing, really. It's all psychological.

I don't use in the daytime because any businessperson can come around and see me. My social worker does pop-in visits—anything can happen—my sister could come to town.

People use daytime for daytime stuff and they use night-time for night-time stuff, so I don't get high in the daytime. They can offer me till they're blue in the face and I'll say no.

I will never do it on the street.

Why do they make it so obvious here? You go to Edmonton and you don't see crowds of people using. It's a little more discreet because the cops are a little more mean there (*laughing*). In Calgary, they get off the horse and arrest your ass and handcuff you to a telephone pole until the paddy wagon comes if they even catch a flap on you.

Some people don't even think I do drugs.

I smoke drugs sometimes; I don't fix. I did before, and then my boyfriend got murdered.

I may spend a hundred dollars a week now. Before it was ten here, twenty here—but I don't buy it off the street anymore. In a day I'd buy a gram and it would last me 'til tomorrow if I didn't give half of it away (*laughing*). That's a hundred bucks.

Usually, if I buy a gram, I tell my old man to come over and visit me. I'm not really smarter now, but I don't take as much shit. It's different. It's really different. Like, we're really good friends. I phone him and say come over.

I've slowed down on smoking; I never really quit. I don't really use that much. I don't use every day, every hour, every five minutes, every ten minutes. Not even this week. Not for a week and a half, almost two weeks. I think when it's time for me to quit I'm just going to quit. I'm not going to push myself to the point where I'm on edge and I've got to go in.

Those safe injection sites, what are they going to do?

If it's going to be an injection site, how do they know where you buy the dope? And they're standing there fine, and talking to you, and they do an injection—and all of a sudden they're gone! I don't think I could handle that.

It's not going to stop them. They've been doing it for years. They're going to just go where they feel comfortable going. Some people, that's their trip! Whatever, that's their trip.

And what if so-and-so is going out with so-and-so, and they know so-and-so is over at that site, and so-and-so is working [and] doesn't want so-and-so to know that they have money or something? So, it's a good idea, but then ... You have your good points about it, your bad points about it. We'll see what happens.

I never tried methadone. Everybody's juiced (*laughing*). Amazing! I don't even know what that methadone does! I don't know. I see people sell it. I see people stick it in the freezer but I don't know what it tastes like. I don't know what it's supposed to do. My medication is a hundred milligrams just for one pill. Can you imagine someone taking 130 milligrams of methadone a day? Yuck.

If people stick to treatment it's good, but that's not when they go there; they clean up to bribe somebody. They clean up and say, "I'll give you … I'll do anything for you."

Let's say someone's conning somebody out of some money or something. Okay, "I'll do this for you. I'll do this for you if you promise to go to the detox centre."

I'm healthy. I can't breathe but I'm healthy (*laughing*). But this weather, it's funky. It will rain like this today and tomorrow the sun will be shining, shining (*laughing*). I think I'm living on Noah's ark!

I'm gaining weight though, these pills I'm on, my stress things, the side effect is it makes you eat! So. I eat.

I'm Italian and I eat (*laughing*). I'm growing these hips.

I'm okay. If I just stay on my medication and don't think too much about everything then I won't really get too upset.

I just carry on.

My daughter has [an illness], so I just focus on her. And she's doing okay. When I was a little girl, I always wanted an Easy-Bake Oven. Do you think I got it? No. But my daughter wants an Easy-Bake Oven, so I took her to Brentwood Mall. Sure enough, she got an Easy-Bake Oven. Holy macaroni! I mean they're like almost fifty bucks those things! They're just popping up everywhere.

I'm trying to get my certificate so I can maybe get a job next year, my Food Safe and Serving Right ticket.[15] I'm on Disability Two, so I don't know if the government cuts are going to affect me. Apparently, it's supposed to start happening in the next couple of months, so I guess we'll see. That's the government's business. I don't know; there's nothing I can do about it.

I've been a ward of the government since I was a little girl, so I've never had any reason to worry about it.

---

15. This certifies people to work in the restaurant industry.

Leslie: Why do you want to make your story public?

Black Widow: I've led my life the way I've led my life ...
    I don't know if I've made all the right decisions, but I really don't think I'm that bad a person.
    I don't steal; I don't lie. I'm not a selfish person.
    I'm not a self-centred person.
    Maybe when I'm gone, maybe somebody can read something about me.

But in the meantime-and-between-time, when I'm not working at [three local agencies], when I'm sitting at home, I don't fix dope. I'm not out to hurt anybody. I don't think I'm all strung-out.

Who do you want to read your story?

Well, I don't really know my daughter because—whatever, whatever, because—but maybe she can sit down one day and read about her mom's life.

Four

ANNE

EDITORS' INTRODUCTION

Anne's story begins with recollections of youthful optimism. Of course, the dreams that inspire any eighteen-year-old's ambitions are rarely fully realized, but mental illness is a cruel thief of possibility, severely inhibiting one's ability to recover from life's inevitable disappointments. Add poverty to the mix, and the care, support, and opportunities necessary to enable people suffering from mental illness to live creative and contributing lives are effectively curtailed. Anne's account relays a journey experienced by many poor, mentally ill women living in Downtown Eastside Vancouver: one setback after another, each constituting another brick in a fence that eventually becomes a wall, each consecutive effort to scale or dismantle the wall that much harder than the last.

Anne's stories of loss, conflict, and loneliness are unique neither to her nor to other impoverished and mentally ill women. Kimberly Rogers was a forty-year-old woman who lived in Sudbury, Ontario. She was charged and found guilty of welfare fraud after admitting that she had received both a student loan and provincial income assistance when, in an effort to obtain marketable employment skills, she enrolled in college courses. In August 2001, six months pregnant and under house arrest, Rogers was confined to a small rented room where she committed suicide by taking an overdose of anti-depressant medication. Like Kimberly Rogers, thousands of women in Canada are confronted by circumstances that render hope elusive. Mothers who, like Anne, suffer with mental illness are particularly vulnerable to the corrosive effects of poverty, isolation, and fear.

A subsequent coroner's inquest into the circumstances surrounding Rogers's death made two key recommendations: first, that social assistance rates be raised to reflect the real cost of living so that women like Kimberly would not be forced to break the law in order to survive; second, that the Government of Ontario reconsider its policy of denying social assistance for life to anyone ever convicted of welfare fraud. The second of these recommendations has been implemented; the first has not.

During the years 2000 to 2003, while researchers were recording Anne's stories, social assistance rates in British Columbia were further reduced to well below subsistence levels; services for mentally ill people were cut back; disability allowances were decreased; and many educational supports for children living in low-income families were withdrawn. Anne describes her struggles to secure basic human needs (food, shelter, compassion, respect, and dignity) for herself and for her child—struggles that occur within the context of a society that cares less and less, and social policies that punish more and more. Her needs are clearly articulated, her aspirations modest, her resilience inspiring. Her questions to the non-poor remain unanswered.

Making Dreams Come True ...

Edited from interviews conducted July 2001–March 2002
Interviewer: Dorothy Chunn

My name is Anne. I live on the east side of Vancouver. I am a survivor of incest and sexual assault and a consumer-survivor—of the mental health care system. I have lived in poverty most of my adult life and hope that this part of my life story will help you to understand what it's like to recover from trauma, cope with mental illness, and raise a child—all while living in poverty. I am now in my mid-forties.

I was born on Vancouver Island and then moved to the North Shore when I was about eleven. I've lived in the city of Vancouver since I turned twenty-three.

I graduated from high school and my sister lived in a logging camp, so I went and stayed with her and her husband and I got a job for a month as a kitchen aide. They flew me in and flew me out, so I didn't have to pay for any of that. They wouldn't hire a woman permanently because they didn't have women's quarters and they didn't want any hassles. After a month they found somebody else, so it was just a temporary job. Nobody really explained that to me, but it was just fine because after a month I'd had enough anyways. I basically had $1,500 free and clear, so that was good money because tuition for college then was only $250 a semester. My mom gave me a car, and I earned enough money to get the car on the road, pay my tuition, and have a little bit of spending money.

I can't remember what I worked at after that, but I probably did some kind of work to make a bit of money. That was the year I was seventeen going on eighteen.

College was really fine, I had new friends and a lot of fun learning, but I used to think, "Well, what's the point of this? I'm getting an arts degree and what am I going to do with that?" You know?

Nobody in my family had graduated from university so nobody sort of thought, "Oh, yes, she should go and get a liberal arts degree and then do this or do that." Nobody really had any idea.

It was just my idea that I wanted to go to college, and my mom encouraged us. She'd done a nursing program so she had the idea that we should all have a better education, but she didn't really have any idea of what form that would take. So I did my year of college and then I sort of thought, "What's the point?"

I didn't do so well; I only got Bs, and I thought, "Well, I'm going to get a job."

I went and I got a job working as a clerk. I had a really good supervisor so I got to do a lot of interesting things and I met a lot of really interesting people. I worked for law offices before, so I got to understand economics and business. We had economists that worked for us and we had labour relations people that worked for us, so I got a bit of understanding of how that all operates and a lot of the stuff that goes on behind closed doors, which was kind of interesting.

I was just a clerk there, it was interesting but I was fairly naïve, and I really didn't know who it was that I was working for, what their purpose was. As I've come to understand, their purpose is lobbying. But at that time, it was just an interesting office with interesting people. I had a good job, I made enough money, and I was treated fairly well because I worked very hard.

I saved enough money to go to Australia.

I did a youth exchange program, where you can work on a travelling visa. I worked at McDonald's in Australia and then at an airline company as a clerk, which was an awesome job because it was dead easy. It was a government job; they just needed warm bodies. I worked about three or four hours a day or something like that (*laughing*). It was not strenuous. I'd done clerical work before I left, and it was the same kind of work. I was just sitting at the desk answering the phone, just taking messages, and we had a tea break of fifteen to twenty minutes. You always had a break every morning and every afternoon, you had an hour for lunch, and the office was air-conditioned. At the end of the week we got our pay in cash; they would make up pay packets and hand them out Friday afternoon.

Oh, it was an awesome job; it was really cool!

My mom had cancer and my sister phoned and said I had to come back to Canada because they didn't want to look after her. She was better by the time I got back, but there was nobody in the house. I'm the middle child so I was the one that sort of did everything. My mom had cancer before I left and then she was better, so I left thinking it was over. I didn't have an understanding of cancer.

It came back and she was really sick. I told her I'd be gone a year, but I had in my mind that I would phone around Christmas and say, "Sorry, I'm not coming home. I'm 24,000 miles away so, you know, you're going to have to live with it." (*Laughing*)

You know, that was my intention.

I'd planned a trip to Southeast Asia. I had a ticket around the world from here to Australia to Asia to Europe and back to Canada. I'd planned to travel for the next two or three years and work my way around the world. But my mom, it was inconceivable to her that a twenty-year-old could do that, especially one of her kids. It was just, you know, I mean she never travelled anywhere really; she ended up going to Hawaii and down to Mexico, but I don't think she ever did a road trip across Canada or anything like that, so it was just inconceivable that I could be so far away.

It was fine to think of me in Australia, but to think of me travelling for years was too scary for her. I didn't tell her that I hitchhiked across Australia from Perth to Sydney until I came home.

I thought, "If I don't go back and she dies, could I live with myself?" The answer was "No" (*laughing*). When she was first diagnosed I was nineteen years old and she had been given six months to live. It was mesothelioma of the pleural lining of the lungs, so it's a rapid-growing cancer, but she managed to survive for six years. She lived six years and they gave her six months. But I just sort of thought, "Oh, she kicked it and she's fine." You're twenty; you don't really think about stuff like that. I turned twenty-one in Australia, which was great because they give big celebrations.

So when I came back, the idea of my mom being sick and possibly— you know, at some point I knew she wasn't going to live long. So it wasn't like I could say, "Oh, I'll wait three or four years and then when my mom feels better I'll go." I knew it was a finite time, so I really couldn't keep my money and plan to go travelling again—you know, come back for a month or six months or whatever. So, I had to change my plans. I basically gave up my dream of travelling.

I came back and I lived at home. How long did I live at home? For about another sixteen months. I house sat and did other stuff so I didn't really *live* at home; I hadn't really been connected with my family since I was about eighteen because I worked a lot. We didn't do anything together as a family—maybe holidays, dinners, and stuff like that—but I had my own life. Often, I wouldn't see them because they'd get up at a certain time and I'd get up at a different time and come home late. So, a week could go by where I didn't see anybody. I went to college and I specifically organized my college schedule so that I would get up after everybody left and come home after everybody went to bed.

Basically, I didn't see them because there was too much alcohol, emotional tension, violence, and anger and all kinds of stuff going on in the house. I just didn't want to be part of it anymore; I don't know how conscious it was, but I just coordinated my schedule so that, for most of the week, I never saw my family.

I have five siblings. When I was going to college, my older brother and sister had moved out, and so there was three kids at home, including me. The two younger ones were going to school. My mom and dad both worked and were both early risers, so they would be in bed by nine or ten. I'd get home around ten thirty or whatever and everybody would be in bed. I lived in the basement so I just kind of did my own thing. On weekends I had to do housework and stuff like that, do chores.

When I came back from Australia I worked at other clerical jobs. I had a job working for a company that did IQ testing to determine which applicants qualified for the position. I was one of the people that tested with a really high IQ. That's how they hired people to do the job, which was weird to me because it wasn't a very challenging job; it was just taking orders for construction supplies. But anyway, they said that I had one of the highest IQs of any of the people that they'd tested. I thought that was kind of surprising because nobody had ever tested me during school.

I hadn't had a good experience in high school. I was bullied and ridiculed by my peers and ignored by my teachers. No one had ever suggested I was capable of university. I was stunned. I can't remember what happened with that job, but they hired us for the summer, then they decided to lay us off after about six or eight weeks. I thought, "You know, this is going to be the routine if I'm a clerk. I don't have any particular skills; I can be hired and fired at will. I don't have anything I can bargain with. I'm not part of a union." So I decided to go back to school.

My mom had worked as a nurse and she had to do shift work, which was really hard. She thought that the ultimate job would be to be a therapist because they work Monday to Friday and have regular hours. I actually kind of wanted to be a writer and go to Ryerson, but there was no support in my family to do something like that. When I went to the counselling office to find out about the program, they said, "Oh, you're not bright enough, you'll never make it in."

I'm just, like, "Well, fuck you."

My first year in university I had an 80 per cent average, but because my average had been so low in college, when they transferred my credits to the university, my average got lowered to around 75 per cent. My next year, I had a couple of profs in second-year psych who knew the whole scheme.

The law students all had to take psychology courses and general arts, and the health sciences students had to take them too. They knew that it was based on marks, so if you did an extra essay you'd get ten extra marks. I think on one of my courses I had a hundred and forty-five out of a hundred and fifty because I did a couple of extra essays and got extra marks for that. So I ended up with a really good average that was adequate for me to get into the counselling degree program. The first year I applied I didn't get in. The second year I applied I got in. Only thirty-six people were accepted out of 300 applicants. I had done all my prerequisite courses, so it made my first year in the program a lot easier. That was good; my mom was really pleased and happy for me.

Then my mom died in my first year of the program, and they didn't give me any counselling or support, so it was really awful. I realized that I could either continue or bail, but that if I bailed I'd probably not complete the program and it would be really hard to get back to it next year.

Mom died towards the end of my first semester, just before exams. I just thought, "I'm just going to do them." I did as many exams as I could. There was a medical terminology exam, but I said, "Well, that's just a waste of time, I can do that anytime."

I said, "I'm not going to do this, I'm not going to do that. I'm going to study for these eight exams, the other two I'll put off until after Christmas."

But I had to write all of them, even the medical terminology, which was a total bullshit course. And they didn't say, "Oh, well, you've got nine out of ten on your assignments, let's just not worry about that; obviously we can just average your marks."

They didn't let me defer any of the exams. I had to write them all and I got no counselling, no support. But I somehow just caught up and just kept working. Then in my final year—like a lot of final-year students—I almost had a nervous breakdown.

We had to do a thesis for our final year in the program, and I couldn't put it together. I mean I kind of put together a half-assed sort of thing. I did some of the research, but I didn't have a very coherent thesis and I didn't have a plan, and nobody said, "Well, you know, that doesn't seem really coherent," or, "What's your research?"

Nobody supervised us, so I just did the best I could and basically almost failed. But I passed everything else and I'd had an 80 per cent average, so they just let me go. I was about this close to having a nervous breakdown because of the stress of having my mom die and working so hard at university.

In the program, we had to do a practicum. My first practicum, they put me in the hospital that my mom had worked at—where everybody knew her and knew that she'd died. It was horrible, and nobody said, "Oh, gee, that's not such a smart idea." You know?

Nobody really cared about who we were. It seemed all they cared about was our marks.

The year before I graduated, they paid people to do their final internships. As an intern, you have a 75 per cent caseload and you're basically assisting. You might not be as qualified as a regular therapist but you're going to be graduating in a couple of months and working at a full rate of pay. There used to be a thousand-dollar-per-month stipend so that people could do their internship. The year that I graduated, they cut out that program. I had to borrow money to complete my internship so that I could graduate with my bachelor of science. But I couldn't work until I completed these two, month-long internships, and I couldn't complete them without this money. I had to borrow money for four months so that I could labour in the hospital for free!

I got through all that, graduated, and decided that I really was interested in a further specialization, so that's what I ended up doing. I ended up working with a woman who was an excellent manager and supervisor—really supportive, really fun, very pleasant to work for. I worked with her but they didn't have any full-time positions. I worked at another hospital, and my boss there was really flaky. For one of the first times I was making a reasonable income—more than enough to pay my rent. I had a huge student loan though, and it took about 25 per cent of my income. My rent was about 40 per cent of my income at that time. I had a good job, a nice apartment, a boyfriend, and things seemed to be okay. I had believed at that time that I would graduate, work, and get married et cetera, et cetera.

I had moved out of home when I went to university and got my own apartment—a bachelor's suite in a house. I lived there until I finished school, and then my boyfriend said, "You know, we'd do much better if we were in a bigger place." So, we decided to get a bigger place. I had another year where we were kind of dating and hanging out, and then he went on a holiday and said he wasn't coming back.

My boyfriend left and I fell apart.

I had my first mental health breakdown in 1986, after I had been working as a therapist for a year and a half.

I hadn't really dealt with any of my history of childhood incest and sexual abuse, alcoholism and violence. I hadn't really dealt with anything. I just kind of kept moving, and it never quite caught up to me. My mom's death—never dealt with any of that kind of stuff until this final event, and then I just couldn't carry on. It all just caught up to me, all at the same time. It was like I tried to outrun it and I couldn't.

I was diagnosed with manic depression, and they put me on one of the major tranquillizers. They put me on Thorazine, a very small dose, but I was just whacked. A very small dose of Thorazine—it really amazed me because I'd worked with clients that were on Thorazine.

My God! If sixty milligrams of this just completely whacks me out, what does 200 milligrams do for them?

I just felt nothing, couldn't even think, and my psychiatrist wouldn't deal with my childhood issues of incest. I wasn't hospitalized then, but all my colleagues had worked in mental health so very few of them were willing to stay in contact. There was one woman that I kept in contact with, but the rest of them, like my supervisor and most of the people that I worked with were, like, "Now you've crossed to the other side."

They didn't say anything; they just never kept in touch. I didn't really have a lot of support. Yeah, it was 1986, and people were freaked out, you know?

I stopped taking my medication because it just made me feel numb inside. I had no money so I stayed with different people until I could get my unemployment benefits.

I couldn't work. I'd had a nervous breakdown.

It wasn't like they said, "Oh, well, why don't you take a six-month leave, get counselling, get support, and then see if you can come back to work?" You know, do like a long-term disability thing, right? I don't know if they had long-term disability. If I had been there long enough, I should have had some kind of disability, but nobody said, "Why don't you do this, or this"; nobody took me aside the way they would have if I'd had some other kind of illness, like if I'd been in a bad car accident or something like that. I didn't know what to do, so I went on medical UI and then they just basically gave me my superannuation and sent me off. That was it.

I lived in another apartment on Commercial Drive. I lived there until I couldn't afford the rent. I couldn't get my UI; I had to wait three months for it to come through or something like that. My mother had died and my father lived in an RV. I had very little family support. I couldn't live on welfare, which was about $300 a month. My income was not enough for me to rent my own place. I had no place to stay, so I lived with a brother for a while, stayed with some friends, did this and that; finally, my UI came through and I could afford shared accommodations. I found shared accommodation out by the university, and it was nice. The other people were doing their PhDs, had their master's degrees, so it was a very interesting group, and I had the basement to myself. For the first year that I lived there, nobody really worried about the fact that I wasn't working. I had my own income and I came and went as I pleased and that was fine. I think I lived there for about three years altogether.

My roommates were busy working or going to university, and for the first two years, everything went well. I felt okay for a while; then I became suicidal. I didn't tell my roommates because I didn't want to lose my housing. I called the crisis line and ended up going in a program called SAFER. The counsellors there are very skilled. They helped me cope with my feelings of suicide and my childhood history of incest and sexual abuse, neglect, family violence, and alcoholism. The counsellor there saved my life.

I was there for a year; they can only work with people for six months to a year. Luckily, after that I was able to find a counsellor who took clients at reduced rates. I paid ten dollars a month and saw her once or twice a month. She helped me function.

In the house where I lived we had three bathrooms; the house was huge and it wasn't a problem for me. I used to just let everyone get up and do their thing; and I slept in late and basically just did my own thing. I was quite depressed but nobody really concerned themselves with anybody else. It was kind of like, "Okay, we're all adults here, we're all doing our own thing."

Then at some point, the guy who ran the house—collected the rents, and whatever—at some point, he just decided that he didn't like me. I don't know what it was about, but he didn't like the fact that I wasn't working. I was paying my rent; there were no problems.

I wasn't causing any problems. I wasn't having parties or anything that would disturb anybody else. Basically, he just didn't like it. He was kind of a bully and I think he just decided to pick on me. He was doing his PhD. He lived there too, but he'd lived there for the longest time and so, ostensibly, he ran the house; but really, he only paid rent the same as anybody else and he wasn't the landlord. The landlord lived next door.

Anyway, he decided that I had to move. It wasn't a matter of, "Let's put it to a vote at our monthly meeting," or "We're not really comfortable with this." There wasn't anything like that. He just came and told me that nobody in the house wanted me, which really quite upset me. But when I actually started checking it out with a few of the other people, that wasn't really true. Then he just made my life uncomfortable. Was I going to stay in this house where I would have to avoid him? That wouldn't have been very comfortable because we shared a kitchen. I just said, "Okay, it's time to move."

This was really distressing.

It took several months to find another place. I was in a cycle of not working and feeling very depressed, and it was hard to find housing.

So I found another shared house, then I had a problem with the person who ran it. These people rented the house and wanted to get some extra rent money, so they rented to me. I had been on UIC up until that point, and then my UIC ran out. I had to get a note from them to get welfare. But the guy who ran the house was flipping cars—buying and selling cars—so I think he was afraid that income tax would somehow get hold of this information. He was really weird about the whole thing. I think he signed the letter, but he was really unhappy about it and he basically gave me notice.

I found another place and, yet again, had the same problem. This time one of the people in the house was really an unhappy person, and every little sound would annoy her. So if you got up in the morning at ten o'clock and started doing the dishes, and she woke up fifteen minutes later, she would say that the noise of the dishes was what woke her. People didn't tippy-toe around, but at nine o'clock in the morning, people should be up or they can sleep through whatever. So it was a little bit of a thing, and after a while she started creating problems for me because, again, rather than deal with her own issues, it was easier just to create problems for me. I moved out of that house and decided, no more shared houses. These had failed three times in a row.

In the last shared house, I became suicidal. It was just so distressing to me to live in shared houses and have people's politics enter my living space. I didn't feel safe anymore because people would scapegoat me, and it wasn't like I could just go into my place and lock the door and that would be that.

I was suicidal in '88. From '88 to '89 I was with a counsellor at SAFER, and then I had a Gestalt therapist until I became ill. She did therapy but she couldn't deal with mental illness, which was beyond the scope of her practice. On the night I planned to kill myself, I wrote a note about my unhappiness and what to do with my things. Then I decided to carry out my suicide plan. But then I thought, "If I can't stand my job, and my living situation is intolerable, why not just leave?" I packed up a few things and left.

I had an aunt who lived on Vancouver Island, so I went to visit her and my cousins. I stayed for the weekend, came back, gave my roommates a month's notice, and quit my job. So, that was it for me. You know, if you're not mentally stable, shared accommodations are really trying. I think they're difficult enough if you are healthy! I think even if you are healthy it's fairly hard to keep it together and have solid roommates and have stability. Let's say that you own your own house and you're renting out a suite in it; you know that you own the house and you're not going to lose it. But if you're the person that's renting and you're renting with other people, it's really not a stable situation. I just thought, "Forget that!" I'd rather live in an SRO downtown and know that I have my own place than live in shared accommodation.

I decided to move away from Vancouver.

I wasn't functioning very well in the city; I had almost tried to commit suicide so I thought I wanted to get out. At first, I had tried living on the island near my sister. I rented a place—my sister's husband wouldn't let me live with her because I was ill. I'd had an abortion and almost committed suicide, and I was very ill.

Eventually, I moved up to the Queen Charlottes and boarded for six months with somebody who was quite nice. There was a lady that boarded people. I was very lucky. I chose to move there because it was just the farthest place from Vancouver I could get (laughing).

I thought, "I'll just go up to the Charlottes, maybe I'll find a place to stay"; and I hitchhiked all the way up. I caught the ferry with my last twenty-five dollars. I asked if there was anyone that would exchange room and board for work, and this woman did that. People could do stuff around the place like chop wood, and she would exchange board for that. So she did that for me. I got a job up there for a couple of weeks and made enough money to get back home, and then I thought, "Well, I'm not really happy here. I don't have any friends." My sister, I see her now and then, but it's not really a strong connection and I really liked this person I met in the Charlottes, so I phoned her and asked her if I could board over the wintertime. My UIC had come through, so I knew I would have enough money. Room and board was only $500 a month, and my UIC was a little more than that. It was a wonderful, spiritual environment. I felt that I had a strong spiritual connection to the Queen Charlottes, and it felt very healing and restorative to be there.

After about six months I became ill again, and there was nobody to treat me, so that's when I came back to Vancouver. The only housing that I could find was in the Downtown Eastside. I lived in SRO housing, but the noise literally drove me crazy. I wound up in a hospital psych unit because it was just too noisy and too deprived. I mean I'd grown up on the North

Shore so I'd been around trees, water, and stuff like that. It was a really deprived environment for me. I found it was just too stressful with the noise and the violence. Our building was safe, but you walk out the door and there's blood on the pavement. People are getting into fights and people are drinking on the street. It wasn't as bad then as it is now; this was '91, I guess. People weren't shooting up right on Hastings Street like they do now, but people were definitely shooting up in the alleyways. Where I lived, the noise was constant and the ambulances were constant. I used to joke that we should just have a triage station right in the middle of Hastings and Main because at least every hour there's an ambulance on that corner. Basically, they should just park one there. Yeah, so, it's noisy and it's stressful because when you hear a siren there's just something about it that says something's wrong, you know?

It was too stressful. I became ill and was hospitalized.

At that time I was going to SARA. The group leader was very kind, she became my sponsor and we are still good friends. At my first meeting, people were talking about how hard it was to pretend everything was normal at Christmas—especially if no one in your family believed your story about incest. I felt better knowing that I wasn't the only person who had a fucked up family, who dreaded Christmas, and who didn't know how to cope. SARA gave me some ideas about how to cope and some people to call. It was a SARA friend who tried to get me some help when I was falling apart. I tried to get into the hospital and get help before I became really crazy. I had been wandering the Downtown Eastside (I lived at Main and Hastings) in bare feet. In 1991 there wasn't as much drug use as there is now so all I did was cut my feet up really bad with broken glass. Still, the first hospital wouldn't help me.

My behaviour became crazier, and no one in my building really knew about mental illness or knew what to do. Eventually, I got into another hospital. For me, I feel that living in the Downtown Eastside literally made me go crazy. There's no grass or green spaces, just blood and violence and people trying to get money to use. I didn't want drugs, so I stayed out of that, and then I became ill.

After two weeks in the hospital, the most I got out of it was talking to one nurse and some of the other patients. I was told I would be discharged. The nurse suggested I got to Triage. I was from the suburbs! I couldn't imagine going to Triage!

By this time, I'd been in a hospital for mental illness and a shelter for battered women. My boyfriend had threatened me and was becoming increasingly violent, so I left him. I had lived in a Downtown Eastside hotel and an SRO. I thought, "No way! I'm not going back there!" I stayed with friends and then lucked out and found a suite in a house in Coquitlam.

I moved out to Coquitlam and I told them I was planning to be a student up at SFU. They weren't really too inquisitive, and they seemed to like me, so I slept in a house that had a suite in it and that was way better than where I lived before. I didn't have a phone, nobody could bug me, and I could just do my own thing—do my own recovery—which I did. I got well enough to go back to work, and then I did one of those pre-employment programs, got a job, got back to work, and was eventually working in my field again making twenty-five dollars an hour. I went from living in the suite to living in my own apartment, and then the stress of a number of different things hit me.

I met somebody and I didn't realize he had a drinking problem; he and his friend broke into a neighbour's house and stole a bunch of booze and some electronic equipment. It didn't even occur to me that anybody would do this. Because of this person who had come to stay with me for a short period, I ended up having to leave. I wouldn't have been kicked out, but they just weren't very happy with me. Again, it was a situation where I could have stayed but they didn't feel safe. I felt really bad about having invited this person into the house. I've had that situation with alcoholics; I don't really think that somebody is an alcoholic because they don't drink around me and I don't drink with them. I don't even know how they found out there was booze. Maybe I left them and they decided to just snoop around or whatever. Anyway, I left there and lived in New West for about a year and a half. I had gotten a job in New Westminster, and then I became ill again. That was in '93.

I found that my job was emotionally draining. When I worked, I became mentally ill. I realized that, basically, the stress and the demands of that kind of position—and the fact that I'm personally not suited for it—all means that it doesn't work for me. When I didn't practise for a year and a half because I became ill, it took me a long time to re-qualify. When I eventually re-qualified, within about six months, I became mentally ill. So, to me it became very obvious that this wasn't working for me. I mean, other people get ulcers and heart conditions and have to change their jobs. Mine caused too much mental distress.

Part of the distress is that I find it very difficult working with people who have lots of problems that I cannot resolve or assist them with. So I feel kind of stuck with these people, and every day I'm exposed to their unhappiness and their inability to manage in the world. That doesn't work for me. I found that I can't work with people specifically. Like, I can help people in a general way, but to sit down with somebody and find out they've been sexually abused as a child, that they were suicidal, and that they'd slashed, and so on ... I don't really want to deal with this. My life is full enough with pain and disaster, and I don't really want to listen to anybody else's stories and feel responsible for doing anything about them, you know? The things that I was trying to do for people I couldn't do. There was nothing that I could—with all my education and with all my abilities—change for them.

Something triggered my sexual abuse issues at work, and this caused me to break down because there was no way of dealing with them there. I didn't feel I could sort of say, "Okay, well, this has triggered my sexual abuse issues," talk to a counsellor, and get some help to see how I could deal with it and arrange my work situation so I could feel safe.

I became ill around Christmas 1993. I was working two part-time jobs at that time for a total of forty hours a week. I decided to quit one job, so I was only working seventeen hours a week and still making $1,400 a month clear. I was managing on that but there was a lot of pressure on me then. They wanted me to have my own car, and I just couldn't manage. I didn't have enough money to buy a car, and they wouldn't let me use the car they had. I ended up using transit, which was adequate. I didn't have that many clients and it wasn't a big deal. But it was an issue for them, and there was a lot of pressure. My supervisor was one of those people who ... I did 75 per cent of the work right, and she'd pick the 25 per cent that I did wrong and that would be what she would emphasize. It was not a style of management that worked very well for me.

So anyway, that job was just too stressful, and I'd had a series of jobs where people did that to me. I couldn't tell them I'd had a mental health breakdown. I told them that I was sick and I couldn't go back to work. I said that the doctor had asked me to take a medical leave and I somehow got a medical letter. I don't know how I did all that from the hospital, but I somehow managed to do all that without admitting that I was hospitalized. I tried to go back to work then found there was too much pressure and I quit for medical reasons.

I moved and my UI got lost, so for a long time I had no UI. On welfare, I had just enough money for rent. So I wasn't eating properly, I wasn't sleeping properly. I had no resources. I wasn't connected to any of the mental health teams and I became psychotic. They gave me Lithium while

I was in the hospital at Christmas, but it made me sick. With me, if I get distressed my adrenal cortex produces far too much adrenaline, sometimes for absolutely no reason at all. This time—1993–94—I had no money for food, I was not sleeping, and I was really distressed. But in recent times my stress has become more endemic; like poverty and inadequate housing and stuff like that. That doesn't really change day-to-day, week-to-week, month-to-month, but every now and then I'll get distressed about it. It's like I know that I can't really do anything about it, but my system will get distressed. I'll have periods of insomnia and I'll be hyper and irritable and anxious because my adrenal cortex is producing all this adrenaline. It's the flight response. I know there's no place for me to run away to and there's nothing that I can do. I'll just take my prescription medication to counteract the effects of the adrenaline so I can function normally. I'm lucky that it works. At this point, I'm taking the same amount during times of less stress, and I have been able to manage with that and still sleep well. I would like not to have to take medication in order to sleep, but, if I don't take it, I don't sleep and I can't function.

So, again, I didn't have any friends, I'd lost my job, and there wasn't really anything out there for me. I was in Al-Anon at that time, and somebody there knew of this really nice cheap apartment in the East End. It was a beautiful apartment with wooden floors and an old tile bathroom. It was lovely, but there was no soundproofing and the person who lived below me was used to having this other person living above her. He'd lived there for twenty years and she'd lived there for fifteen years, so she had gotten used to what time he woke up, what time he went to bed. I was a strange person, and she just didn't cope with it very well. It was the same as that person I had met before. She would phone me at six o'clock in the morning because I got up to go to the bathroom.

"I could hear you going to the bathroom," she would say.

"Yes ... and the problem is?"(*Laughing*)

I wasn't sleeping very well so I would get up in the middle of the night and run a bath. But if I woke up in the middle of the night and heard somebody having a shower or running a bath it wouldn't be, like, "Oh, my God, something is wrong with the neighbours," you know? I would just feel, like, "Oh, okay, someone upstairs is having a bath." In some places that I've lived, quite often you hear people across the way fighting and that kind of stuff. Now that's scary. If somebody fights or parties a lot, then you phone the landlord and deal with that. Anyway, she complained and complained and complained. She didn't complain to me, she complained directly to the owner. Between her complaining and me not eating properly, not sleeping well, and having no real contacts with anybody who was healthy, I became ill. I was very ill that time, psychotic.

In that spring of '94 I had no work, no friends, no family support. My life unravelled. I became psychotic and I was hospitalized in the locked unit for a couple of weeks. I got picked up by an ambulance in another neighbourhood. I was kind of living on the street because I felt uncomfortable in my apartment—I had an apartment but I was out there on the street being crazy. I think you become ill when you don't have anybody to help you. If you were my friend and you saw me becoming ill you would maybe take me to the hospital and say, "She's not acting normally, she's not sleeping, she's not eating."

This is the thing that is insidious about mental illness. I think if you become ill for other reasons people are more comfortable dealing with it. When you become mentally ill, there's a lot of shame and stigma involved. That was a horrible experience. I just totally spun out of control and wound up psychotic and in the hospital. It was really scary. I don't ever want to go to the locked unit again!

That's when I got involved with the mental health team. Their support made a huge difference. I've been seeing somebody every week there and seeing the psychiatrist on a regular basis every two or three months. The psychiatrists mostly just check your meds and make sure you're not psychotic; the case managers help with day-to-day problems and help you to cope. I've functioned well since then, working very actively to keep on top of sleeping, eating, and stuff like that.

I sort of got back on my feet and had a really good psychiatrist who was doing an internship. I saw him for about four or five months I guess, and then he finished his practicum and went on to do something else, but during that time he helped me get settled and stable.

I realized I wanted to have an income, "I've got to take care of myself here. I've got to get on the ball."

After my hospitalization, the landlord wanted me out of that place because I had become ill and the woman downstairs was constantly complaining. I found another apartment and then decided, "Okay, well, I need to do something else. I can't do what I used to do." I decided to go back to school and I took a printing program at a community college. It's creative, and I thought it would be something basic, something not that stressful. By the time I'd started my first couple of weeks of school, I realized I was pregnant. Just before the end of term, I had my baby.

I started going out with my child's father when I moved to the East Side. He was just doing his regular thing, which was to play music, get drunk, party, and get stoned. He is very talented but he has a heroin addiction. I didn't realize that he was still using, and it freaked me out because I don't use and there was the risk of AIDS and stuff like that. I decided I don't really need this, and so I got my life more together. I wasn't living with my child's father at the time I had my baby. Although I'd known him for about ten or twelve years, we'd only been together for about three or four months. His addiction and alcoholism was part of the craziness of my life, part of what caused me to become ill. He wasn't supportive and he wasn't stable. I needed support, stability, that kind of thing. We never lived together, and he was not interested in being part of my child's life. He never called me back when I called to say I was pregnant.

I think what happens when you're mentally ill is you don't have a lot of social supports. Then you get mixed up with people who use drugs because they're sort of in the same milieu as you. You're both poor, you both lack housing, you're both living in the same neighbourhoods and whatever.

So that's how my child's dad and I hooked up. If I'd been working we probably wouldn't have hooked up. But I was unemployed and not doing anything, so I could hang out during his weird hours. He would come home at three o'clock in the morning, and this was no problem.

Then I thought, "Hey, I'm going back to school."

I said to him, "I'm going back to school in two weeks. I need you to stop coming around at two, three in the morning because I can't function and get up to go to school."

He just ignored me, and I said, "Look, okay, that's it. The key, you have to give me back the key." He was living somewhere else.

I said, "You have to give me back the key. I'm not dealing with this; you're not listening to me. You're not respectful. I've got to go back to school. I can't have you doing that."

He just freaked out and got really angry, and he packed up his guitar and made a big deal, and left.

I'm thinking, "Great," because he was creating problems in my life, and about two weeks later I started school and realized I was pregnant. This was the second time I'd become pregnant, and I thought it might be my only chance. The only thing that I'd ever wanted was to be a mom. I kind of wanted to be a writer, but the only thing I'd ever dreamed about, ever since I was a little girl, was to be a mom. I thought I'd grow up, get married, have two kids, live in a house, you know? So this might be my only chance.

I didn't test positive for HIV. I figured, "I'm healthy enough and I'm being followed by the mental health team. This is maybe my best chance now of having a child."

So that was it.

I'd already had one abortion, four years previously. I had the abortion because I wasn't well. I was mentally fragile and I didn't have any support systems, so this time I cobbled together some support systems. At least I had the team at this point. I had the team, I had a counsellor that I saw weekly, and I had a place to stay. Last time I had an abortion, I was staying at a hotel on Vancouver Island. So now I had a stable place, I had support, my ducks were more in a row, and I had friends in the neighbourhood. I've got a few people, not close friends, but people that I knew that were single moms on welfare, so I kind of knew that it was doable. I didn't realize how hard it would be. I just went ahead because I thought it would be my only chance. I thought, "I'm not going to wait until I get married." If I'd waited, I'd be forty-three going on forty-four and still not have a child. It's hard enough at thirty-seven, I couldn't imagine having a child now.

Nobody tried to talk me out of it. The mental health team was very supportive; my psychiatrist was pretty supportive. I was on valproic acid, an anti-seizure medication, for my manic depressive illness. It didn't really have any impact on me, but it's not good for the fetus, so I stopped it as soon as I realized this—about two or three weeks into the pregnancy. I didn't finish my printing course, which was like a piece of cake after going to university. I got scholarships, and it basically gave me something to focus on while I was pregnant. Unfortunately, printing doesn't pay very well. If I was on my own I might have explored a career in it and maybe ended up doing something for a small press, but I doubted that I could make enough money to support the two of us. The people that I went to school with were very supportive. I didn't have family support; I didn't have friends but I had a network of people at school that supported me throughout my pregnancy, which was great. I liked going to school. I was fine throughout my pregnancy and didn't need medication. Everything went well and I had a healthy baby.

Anne wrote the following addendum to her story in June 2003.

The Health & Home Study was done over a year ago, so I'd like to update it. My child is now eight years old. In some ways it's easier—you can talk to an eight-year-old and explain why Mom's tired and can't ... There are lots of "cant's" in my child's life.

I am forty-six now and coping with the early phase of menopause. The medication—hormone replacement therapy—gave me migraine headaches. This last weekend I had a headache for about two days, and it lingered for another two. That's four days where it was all I could do to take care of the basics—the laundry, something to eat.

The guilt I feel is horrible. My child is frustrated that I can't do what other moms do. My energy is very low generally, and no one seems to have any idea why. The doctors don't really care about the quality of our lives. It seems acceptable to be poor, to have enough to eat but not enough nutrition. I've tried several food programs. They give me a handful of half-rotten vegetables and tell me I can cut off the mouldy bits. It's disgusting. I don't want to eat mouldy vegetables. There's no war, no depression, so why do I have to eat rotten vegetables? I can't afford a variety of foods on thirty-five dollars per person per week—that's the allowance. When your child turns seven they cut back your welfare by twenty dollars a month or more, depending on the number of children you have. This year we lost about $100 a month in welfare benefits. That's 10 per cent of my income. It was devastating.

We have a little bit of subsidy so our housing now costs what the Ministry of Human Resources allows. I still have to pay about thirty dollars per month for phone and another thirty for heat. Then there's cable, which is a luxury, I guess, and we pay for laundry. Whatever you do, whatever you buy, it comes out of the limited money you get.

I've been poor most of my adult life, but it's harder as a parent. You can go without but you want your kid to look nice, to go to a movie now and then and have a bike, to play at an outdoor camp. So many things are beyond poor parents now. No dental care, no money for medication. I know a mother who had to borrow someone's inhaler for asthma because she couldn't afford to pay for the hundred-dollar prescription. It's tough, and the cuts keep coming. They are cutting back essential services like funding for mental health advocates who help you with welfare and other services. I feel like it's a litany of complaint. I love my kid. I didn't think I'd have to fight just to get the basics for her.

I think single mothers living in poverty don't exist in the consciousness of the world. We need a bigger presence. We do exist, and we are struggling to raise healthy children who will grow up and be a credit to our society and our community. At this point we're trying to do this with the most minimal resources imaginable.

Single moms who would be better off going to school part-time, being on social assistance, and raising children are now being forced to work at menial jobs just so the system doesn't have to pay them social assistance. That's a Victorian concept, not a twenty-first-century concept.

My belief is that every one of us has an incredible gift to give to the world. For some it's being a good mother; for others it's being a surgeon, the premier, or a prime minister. One of the things I had to justify was accepting welfare for a long period of time. I've been on assistance now for eight years. When you think about it, the government pays doctors, the government pays nurses, the government pays bureaucrats—that all comes out of our tax money too. It takes many, many tax dollars to train specialists. We're willing to pay someone to become a cardiac specialist, a neurosurgeon; we're willing to pay people to be MLAs, premiers, councillors on our local municipal boards; but we're not willing to pay someone to be a mother. We're not willing to invest in motherhood. We're not willing to invest in housing and in educational funding.

Children need recreation. We're not willing to give parents the money for recreation activities. What happens if your child wants to do digital animation? Who's going to encourage children to be what they want? There's no one except possibly their mothers. All the mothers that I know are aware of what their child is good at and are frequently frustrated because they can't do much about it.

I have extended family members who have money. They own their own homes, they have good-paying jobs, and they have no idea how we live. They don't visit me, although I might see them at Christmas. It's pretty bleak. Families don't accept mental illness; they don't want to deal with poverty. They make you feel like you always have your hand out. We lead vastly different lives; they go on vacations, while I had two nights away by myself last summer because if I hadn't I would have ended up in the hospital. The Ministry of Human Resources took about three months to pay the caregiver who did respite. Now there's no one I know who could do respite care. No agency right now will pay for it unless you are in the hospital. It has to be that bad. It's hard on families, on under-resourced parents and kids. I really notice how much better I feel if someone takes us out for a meal, you know, at a place like White Spot, or invites us over for dinner. Then I feel better, I have more patience and I don't feel so alone.

Mental illness scares most people. Some of my extended family are scared to invite me to a wedding or something in case I act crazy. Mostly I haven't been really crazy around my family or friends. I became ill once when I was out with my sister. Actually, I was really ill and I couldn't tell her how messed up I was. I didn't have a counsellor or anyone to talk to. I was behaving strangely, and they kind of understood. Still, family members I hardly know won't have anything to do with me. They've never seen me unravel—that's what it feels like, like my life is unravelling.

Somehow, I've managed to keep it together since I became pregnant. I call a person who understands—another parent—and I get through another day. I don't want to just get through the days; I want a chance to live my life. I believe I'm still growing as a person not just as a parent. I want a chance to grow. How do you grow when the only time you can do anything is between the hours of 9:00 am and 3:00 pm when your kid's at school? My Al-Anon group doesn't pay for childcare. My church doesn't have childcare. Parents need to experience their whole selves—they need to be adults doing adult things with other adults. That's become harder and harder because my illness has left me isolated, either entirely alone or alone with my child. We have no neighbours to visit; there are no support groups where I can meet other parents who are coping with mental illness. For many weeks, the only person who came to our house was the homemaker. She is the only other person my child has seen on a weekly basis since she was an infant.

Of all the issues I have struggled with as a parent, I find isolation to be the most stressful. Without the support of homemakers, daycare and family places and the social opportunities they provide, we would be even more isolated. I can honestly tell you that without the support of a variety of community agencies, including MCF, GVMHS, East Side Family Place, North Health Unit Infant/Toddler Program, the Kettle, and YWCA Single Mothers Group at Kiwassa, I would not have been able to manage. I would probably have had to go to the hospital and my child would have been in care.

When most people look at me, they don't realize that, although we have received some of the support we needed in our community, we have also been stigmatized by things that my child and I have little control over. People don't treat us well because we are on assistance and are poor. They are uncomfortable with the fact that I have a mental illness and that I can't work outside the home. They don't like seeing a mixed-race family. I really get the sense that so few people care about what happens to us. We're disposable. If we make it, fine. If we don't, well, too bad, so sad. They predicted we wouldn't make it. I pray we will. It's not just up to me, though. There are other stakeholders in our lives. They just don't realize it. Sometimes I think about what would happen if we weren't here—if something happened to us. And I wonder if anyone would notice.

Leslie: Why do you want to make your story public?

Anne: I hope people learn that poverty and mental illness are just factors in people's lives; they don't define human beings. They define what I can do sometimes, but they don't define who I am as a person; they don't define my child. That's what people do; they define me. They say you can't possibly be a good mother. Who says?

We know what's safe because we know what's out there. We know the drug addicts; we've been sexually abused. We know the dangers. I think we're much more aware of what can happen, yet we're the ones that are looked upon as fucked up. I know people who are no longer my friends who believe I don't have the right to raise a child that I can't financially provide for. I believe I have that right. I believe that's a human right. It's a right. It's a choice, and people get to make those choices.

I think this whole book of our stories is saying, "We might be recovering addicts, we might be recovering alcoholics, we might be recovering from a number of different things. That doesn't take away anything from our ability to be great mothers." That's what I want people to know. I want people to know that we're intelligent, thoughtful, and insightful people who care for our children. That we're careful with our children. That we do our best to allow them to grow and develop to the extent that they can, even when our growth and development is stunted because of our resources. There's only enough resources for one of us, either the child or the parent, to develop, so it's the child that's going to get the resources and I'm just going to have to live with the fact that this is where my life stops in some ways. I think these are important concepts, important values.

I think single mothers living in poverty don't exist in the consciousness of the world. We do exist. As a society, do we accept that children are valuable? If we accept that children are valuable, then we have to value their mothers. There's a big push to value children, but if they come home to an unhappy mother—someone who isn't cared for and who doesn't have the resources to be a good mother—then it's not going to work.

Who do you want to read this story?

The people I want to read this are people who live outside my milieu—poor single mothers. I don't really associate anymore with anybody else. Middle-class people do not generally associate with poor single mothers. The middle-class women who own their own homes and have their own cars don't form friendships with the single mothers that are on social assistance and that have health or medical challenges. It just kind of separates out. So you end up hanging out with moms who have financial challenges, have health challenges, have challenging or complicated life situations.

I remember meeting a mom and she invited me to this lovely meal with place settings. Really, really lovely. My child and hers were getting along fine; we were having a nice conversation; she was a very intelligent person. Everything was going fine, then she asked where my child's father is, so I told her the truth. I said her father is a heroin addict and that he's not able to participate in our life. That was our last visit there. I wasn't a middle-class mom.

I would like them to know that I am not an incompetent person. I am not an ignorant person. I'm an educated person. I have a pretty good understanding of what parenting requires, and, for the most part, I'm able to provide that for my child. I'm basically as good a mother as you are, with way less resources of every kind—material, emotional, and spiritual. With all those limitations, I still feel that I'm doing a great job mothering.

Even though we have the same concerns, middle-class moms often don't see themselves as being, in any way, shape, or form, the same kind of person that I am. I had the same education as those people, and had I not had a mental illness I would have the same standard of living as they do. In my case, it's kind of like I missed that brass ring because of my mental illness, and so I'm designated down here.

What do you think is the value of telling these stories?

What happens is that they fund group by group. Like, a whole lot of attention is going to people who suffer from cancer—and that's great— but you don't pay a whole lot of attention to people who are suffering from mental health issues, which may or may not be life-threatening. Mental health can be a life-threatening issue if a parent is suicidal. Put these things into perspective; get us on the map.

One of the things that I saw that was significant with the Four Pillars was that it changed Mayor Owen's attitude about drug addicts.[16] Prior to that he had no association with those people, had no understanding of those people. He didn't see how those people were anything like him.

---

16. The Four Pillars is an official approach to citywide drug use adopted by municipal authorities in the United States, the United Kingdom, and Europe. These pillars are: prevention, treatment, enforcement, and harm reduction. A framework for implementing this approach was passed by Vancouver City Council in 2000. At that time, Philip Owen was the mayor.

Somehow, he made a connection with those people. I think that if we can do our stories and that somehow somebody can make a connection with us, then maybe they can also provide us with the resources to really evolve as people and to provide for our children so that they can really evolve.

I don't know if our stories will help, but that's my hope. I need to leave my child a better place to live in. If I don't actively work in my community to change things and make them better, even to some small degree, then I believe that, as a parent, I'll have failed.

Five

SARA

EDITORS' INTRODUCTION

In "Dust Yourself Off, Pick Yourself Up," Sara speaks frankly and courageously about her life, including her relationships with her children. Her mothering is complicated by her own early history as well as by the circumstances and experiences of her adult life. She describes the dilemmas she faces in dealing with the challenges encountered by many parents: how to make the best decisions for the welfare of children in the context of available options. Seldom are these simple or straightforward choices. We urge you to read Sara's stories about mothering alongside other, perhaps more familiar, parental accounts.

In the midst of war or extreme hardship, for instance, parents sometimes surrender their children to the care of others who can offer peace, food, and the possibility of a secure future. Stories about such tragedies often move more fortunate people to lament the painful choices faced by parents who are victims of human cruelty and avarice. Sara's mothering is not impacted by bombs, troops, or famines. Rather, the options Sara chooses concerning the welfare of her children are shaped by being poor, female, and troubled in contemporary Canada.

Sara's stories could also be read together with those of more privileged Canadians, including those who develop and enforce social policies that significantly shape the lives of women like Sara. Wealthy parents, for example, may send their children away to boarding schools to provide them with the education and discipline they hope will ensure their stability when they reach adulthood. Parents striving to succeed in competitive professions may employ full time nannies to provide the care they do not. Those who enjoy travel and who crave romance and excitement—which sometimes includes illicit drug use—may pay for supervised vacations to protect their children from the dangers generated by parental indulgences. News of private childcare and elite recreation does not fuel moral panics or accusations of taxpayer exploitation. Impoverished mothers who use drugs and/or engage in the sex trade, however, are frequently demonized by the media and politicians.

In rapidly changing times like ours, it often seems as though there are no continuous historical or cultural themes. Rushing to judge mothers and mothering, though, displays unusual historical resilience and cross-cultural resonance. Like all parents, Sara may make decisions the consequences of which her children may suffer. However, the wisdom of choices can only be judged in the context of available options. Rare is the parent unencumbered by any regret. Judgment of others, after all, is best made in front of a mirror.

Dust Yourself Off, Pick Yourself Up

Edited from interviews conducted May 2001–January 2002
Interviewers: Denielle Elliot and Cathy Chabot

I was born on Vancouver Island. When I was a newborn we moved to Ontario, then, shortly after, we moved to Alberta.

My dad wasn't very educated; he quit school in Grade 8 or something. We moved out to Alberta so he could work and then he started going to school, so my mom supported the family. He kind of took odd jobs here and there, so we moved where the work was. My mom worked in an office and waitressed, but mostly she worked in an office.

When I was about four, just before I started kindergarten, we moved back to the Coast. I went to kindergarten there and half of Grade 1, then we moved to northern B.C. I stayed there until I was in Grade 5 and then we moved again and stayed there until I was thirteen or fourteen. My parents got separated, so my mom and me and my brother moved to Calgary and stayed there for a couple of months, then I moved back to the Coast to live with my grandparents for a year or so. My dad was going to counselling then. He said I couldn't live with him, so I went to live with my grandparents. When I was at the end of my fourteenth year, I moved to Alberta to live with my mom again. I stayed there until I was fifteen, and then I moved into a foster home in a nearby town.

My parents got separated because of sexual abuse, with my dad. Even though what my dad did was wrong, I felt so sorry for him because he was all alone. We left him, and my mom wouldn't tell him where we were, so I phoned him. That's why I was only with my mom for a couple of months, because she found out that I was talking to my dad on the phone and she kicked me out of the house. I lived with my mom but she was physically violent and very mentally abusive, so that didn't work; that didn't work, and I was out of there.

It's illegal to run away from home in Alberta. They put you in juvie for that, so they put me in juvenile detention. I told them that if they were going to put me back with my mom I'd just keep running away, so they might as well just do something else with me (*laughing*). Foster homes, that was okay—better than living at home.

My foster family, they had bucks. He managed a business that was the big thing in town, pretty well everybody thrived off it. They were really good people and they weren't in it to make any bucks off the kids or anything. If I had stayed there, even after they didn't get money for me from the government, they were going to put me through college and buy me a car. They were really good people, but I was too busy doing my own stupid stuff. They had two kids of their own, two boys and another girl—my foster sister. We got really close, actually; she had already lived there for a couple of years. She was a year older than I was, so we kept in contact.

I lived with them for two years when I wasn't busy running away (*laughing*). Who knows why! It was probably one of the best things that ever happened to me, but I was too busy screwing around.

I was abused from a really, really early age. Like, I don't even remember when it started. Not from my dad, but from my grandfather and my mom's and dad's best friend's son. So by the time my dad abused me, I was, like, ten or eleven years old, and it just seemed—normal. I just thought that's the way it was.

As you get older, you just know that it's wrong, and I got to the point where I was really sick; I'd eat and I'd throw up. I couldn't hold down food. I was a really good student; I had an A to B average. My life was very sheltered because of our religion. I poured a lot of myself into my schoolwork. I did really well and I never skipped out; it never even crossed my mind. But I was so sick that I couldn't go to phys. ed. anymore. I was fainting and I hid in the bathroom (*laughing*), I'd skip out and hide in the bathroom.

So they sent me to a counsellor because they thought I was taking drugs!

I started seeing a counsellor for a couple of months and I didn't tell her about the abuse. One day she was having a meeting with my mom, and I just knew I was going to get a beating when I got home because I was just being a bad kid, right? So what I did was, I wrote her a letter and told her everything and I asked her if she would please tell my mom. And she didn't.

When I got home that night ... as soon as I walked in the door, my mom started dragging me around and slapping me. I told her out of spite because she was hurting me and I wanted to hurt her back. After I told her, when we finally sat down and talked, I asked her if the counsellor said anything to her, and she hadn't. She phoned the school and she wouldn't let me go back there.

That's how it came out.

There was abuse very early that I didn't remember until I started going to counselling. That didn't come out for a couple of years after that.

My mom was *convinced* that I was smoking pot, drinking, and doing drugs. I was drinking but I was not doing drugs. She sent me to a drug and alcohol counsellor, who went, "No, you don't need drug and alcohol counselling, but I'm going to send you to Rape Relief."[17] They hooked me up with a counsellor for a while. Then, when I went to my foster home, they put me in extensive counselling as well as counselling with my mom—who brought a social worker with her! To counselling! I don't know if she was afraid that something was going to come up. You might as well bring your lawyer!

I know that she knew about the sexual abuse when I was growing up— I mean, it was her father. Her father abused her for years while she was growing up and then he abused me. So I know damn well that she knew. She walked in on my dad in my room one night, so she can't deny it, but she just chose not to see it because she hadn't dealt with her own issues. I think she was afraid of any legal issues that might have come about because she was really pushing me to charge my dad and I wouldn't do it. I wasn't into it either way. It wasn't going to change anything.

We don't speak.

I ended up getting ulcers partly because of religion. When you get kicked out of the church they called it being "disfellowshipped." So my dad was disfellowed. He was trying to get back in, so he was still going to church, but nobody was allowed to speak to him. Nobody, not even his mom and dad, unless he was living with them. The only people that are allowed to talk to you are your immediate family.

I'm the black sheep of my family for not going to church. I never hear the end of it. Thump me over the head with a Bible!

I hate religion now; I just hate it with a passion.

I believe we didn't get here by ourselves, but I don't know how, I don't know why. Obviously something more intelligent than we are got us here,

---

17. Feminist organization dedicated to the eradication of violence against women. It offers shelter for battered women, a twenty-four-hour crisis line, and support groups.

but other than that, I don't believe. I just believe there's something that I don't know, that's all.

I wouldn't even bother to check into religions because I just hate them that much. I just think you die. Yeah, that's it, and it's over with. It would be nice if it wasn't, but it's better to believe in the worst and not be disappointed, right?

I went to live with my dad for a summer when he got married. My dad and I both went through lots of therapy and we actually get along really good now. What's the past is the past, and you've got to leave it there I guess.

I didn't like his wife. It was her home, "their" home, she made that plain, so I didn't stay there. I had to ask before I got anything out of the fridge. Seventeen years old and I had to ask if I could get a glass of milk!

No, I don't think so.

I stayed there for the summer and for the wedding and all that, and then I went back to Alberta and moved in with the guy that I was dating. We spent the summer just before I turned eighteen in Vancouver, then we came back and I left him.

I stayed in Alberta for a little while, but I just turned eighteen and I couldn't get welfare there because you had to be nineteen. So when I left him I was screwed; I didn't have anywhere to live, and I was drinking a lot—that was my priority.

I met this girl going to the bar and I went and stayed with her. She had two kids and she let me stay at her place and told me how she got money. Well, she was on welfare, but she used to go every couple of weeks to Edmonton and work the street for the weekend. That was her way to survive. So I went with her one weekend and I never came back (*laughing*).

I stayed in Edmonton for a couple of months and I got picked up by a pimp there. He was treating me really bad; so another pimp took me to ————. I lived there for another few months and then I met another working girl, who was coming to Vancouver, and she said, "Well, you can come out here and work for yourself and you don't have to pay anybody."

So I came out here. I moved here to avoid working for a pimp.

In Alberta, basically, you had to work for somebody unless you wanted to go work the slums, like here. I came with another working girl who was actually a trannie, but better-looking than a lot of women I know, that's for sure!

We came up here and she mostly worked because she had been here before and she knew the ropes. I only worked a few times. I was basically a newcomer to working anyways, and she felt protective of me. She got picked up by the kiddie cops for being underage and I was stuck here all by myself, didn't know a soul.

I had to go to work, but I didn't work for very long. I met some other people and they introduced me to a welfare worker. I was still underage, but because I had been on my own for so many years, they made an exception and put me under care to live on my own.

Then I got pregnant.

We moved around a couple of times, but I tried to stay in one place as long as possible. The only reason we actually ended up moving was because there was something wrong with the buildings. The place I moved into just before I had my son ended up having cockroaches, so I had to move. We moved into the first floor of a house, and we stayed there until he was six months old.

Then we moved out to White Rock for a while. I moved out there because I thought it was a better place to raise my child, more family-oriented. I swear it's more violent out there than it is here! It was actually a really nice apartment building. It had a pool and a playground and it was a really nice complex, but I was having a lot of trouble with his dad because he started using and I freaked out. I didn't want it in the house. I was vacuuming one day—that was when heroin was in capsules—and I found one in the carpet.

I just lost it! So we had to move back here to get away from him.

We moved to [an East Vancouver suburb]. The day I was moving my stuff in I heard people in the hall talking about the stabbing that happened the night before. I was, like, "No, I don't want to live here." Most of the places we lived were nice because I was really picky, but you can't always tell about certain things—like cockroaches.

My son is asthmatic, same as me—so they say you shouldn't live in a place ... Well, who wants to live in a place with cockroaches anyway? They carry dust, germs, and stuff like that. We did a couple of moves; pretty well, all the places we stayed in were secure buildings, buzzers to get in the door kind of thing.

Then we moved into another house, a main floor and basement, and I actually thought it was going to be the place that we were going to stay for a really long time. It had a nice big yard and right across the street was a park and a pool and everything.

But it had rats in the basement, so I had to move out.

From there we got a house down here in the Downtown Eastside—a really, really nice house—but the area sucked. I opened the door one day—my son was standing right behind me—and this broad is standing there fixing under my porch light! Luckily, he didn't see that, but he was going to run into it sooner or later.

That's when things started. I started using.

He went and stayed with his dad for a bit, and then went out and stayed with my mom.

My son is a teenager now. I had him until he was six.

We were living in [an East Vancouver suburb], which wasn't too bad, better than here. I took him to school one day and there were used condoms on the playground, so I didn't want him down there anymore. He lives with—well, I call her my mom because she thinks of me as her daughter. I actually met her because I was underage when I was pregnant and they gave me a one-to-one worker to take me to my appointments and help me find a place to live. We just got really close. She ended up being my labour coach, and my son used to go visit her every couple of weeks to give me a break. It was supposed to be a temporary thing, but it didn't end up that way.

So that's where he lives now.

He's lived with her since he was six, up in the British Properties area. Not so bad, a better place than where we were living.

I always tried to shelter him from the things that were going on, working, and the drugs and stuff, but he knew that something was going on. Even going to the bathroom I'd say, "You're not allowed in the bathroom when I'm in the bathroom." He knew there was something wrong, so it was better for him not to be there.

It was one thing after another, so he's staying there permanently now. It was the best thing for him and that was what was important.

I did go to see him at first; I'd see him regularly. He'd come stay on the weekend. But I'd start to go on binges. I'd be really good for a couple of months and then I'd binge, and then I wouldn't call because I felt guilty. It was hard on him, even in the good times, because he always was under the impression that he was going to come home. Every time I'd come and pick him up on the weekend, he figured he was coming home so he'd act up and then I'd bring him back.

For his own well-being I made the deal with her that I wouldn't contact him. I talked to her all the time, but I wouldn't contact him personally until I'd been clean and stable for a while.

So I don't see him.

I just hopped everywhere since then, mostly hotels, houses here and there. I lived in one hotel—don't leave your coffee out for more than two seconds unless you want the cockroaches to drink it! I swear all the bugs in there were addicts. It's true! I swear the mice in there were going through withdrawal. You leave your stuff—and this isn't any cocaine paranoia or delusions—I'm telling you, the dope really did go missing! You'd put it in a certain spot where the mice couldn't get it and they'd eat the paper!

A couple of times I moved out of the neighbourhood. I was living with one of my tricks for a while—so that obviously wasn't going to last forever. I moved back down here, and then I moved in with another date and out to the Fraser Valley, but it was just too inconvenient for me to get back and forth. So I moved back here again. Mostly, it's just been hotel hopping, getting a house or apartment for a short time or sharing with somebody. I shared a couple of apartments with people who didn't pay their rent; we got evicted for this, or we got evicted for that.

Now I'm here.

I have never felt safe anywhere I've lived here. I permanently sleep with pepper spray. I tried to move out of the area a few times to clean up and get it together, but I always moved back down here. At least this time I don't feel like I've *ended up* down here; I chose to come to where I am now. Yeah, I'm okay with it now because I didn't come down here to use, I came down here because it's close to all my appointments.

I'm living in a hotel now. At least it's clean—no bugs, no lice—the walls need to be painted though. I'd do it myself, if I could get them to let me do it. I lived here years ago and they've cleaned it up, so it's okay. I'm on the fourth floor where most of the staff, or people that work, live. So it's quiet. They let me move up there because that's where I lived the last time. There's heat and hot water but no bathroom. There's a sink and they have maid service once a week. They don't come in and vacuum or anything; you have to put your sheets inside the pillowcase, outside your door, and if you don't put them out there, tough luck. You've got to vacuum your own room, stuff like that. But it's clean; they vacuum all the stairwells everyday. The elevator's broken and I have to walk up four flights of stairs.

I had to carry all my stuff up four flights—four flights back down, four flights back up. I was just dying.

If I hadn't been working, I wouldn't have been using.

I can say that for a *fact*.

I ended up with HIV and hep C, so it affected my health drastically.

In 1995, I lived with another girl. She came over one day and told me that she was positive. Her and I used to share rigs sometimes. It's stupid judgment. We had lived together for so long that I figured that she wouldn't be sharing with anybody else. Well, it was my own stupidity.

I got tested for about a year, off and on. I got really sick and they put me in the hospital, but they didn't know what was wrong with me. I had a high fever, so high that I was shaking uncontrollably, and it just came on all of a sudden. So they brought me in to the hospital. I stayed there for a couple of days, and they ran a whole bunch of tests on me. When I first came in, they figured, "Oh, well, she's positive," and I said, "Well, no, I just got tested and I was negative." So they ran a whole bunch of tests and they still didn't find anything. I left about three days later, and they still said, "Well, we don't know what's wrong with you."

They took a bone marrow sample, and finally, a couple of months later, the doctor told me to come in and said that I was positive.

It took that long, like, all those tests, and it still came out negative. But, you know? You just know that there's something wrong.

My health has probably been better than it ever has been. I know a lot of people who have been diagnosed after I was and who are a lot sicker and on meds. I just got my count done a month ago and they still say I don't have to be on medication yet. Your count—they try to keep it so that when your count goes down to a certain level, like under 200, then they start you on anti-retrovirals—HIV meds. They don't want to start you too soon, so you have to keep tabs on your count, or get it done so often so that they know when to start you. You don't want to start when you're healthy because it causes so many side effects. You know, you hear about people that are getting really sick and nauseated, constipated or diarrhoea, and it's a living nightmare.

I've got this big thing about my hair; your hair falls out. I'm, like, "Yeah, well, you're not giving me any of that pill!"

I went in to get my meth prescription and the nurse said, "Oh, you're really wheezy and you better go see the doctor, I don't like that cough."

I'm like, "Yeah, yeah, I know."

But she's not going to give me antibiotics because we've got an agreement that she will only give them to me if it's absolutely necessary because, as I get sicker, I'm going to need them. If I use them up now, I'm screwed later.

I've never really felt effects from the HIV—maybe being tired and stuff like that, but I've never really been sick. For the last couple of days both of my big toes have been numb on the side and underneath. It's not from my shoes or anything because I've been wearing sandals. Then last night they started ... you know how your feet fall asleep, and, when they wake up, they burn and prickle? But they're still numb, and that's a sign of neuropathy, which is ... I don't know, exactly. One of the common things that happens to people that are HIV positive—the fingers or the toes, they go. Some people experience it very slightly and some people experience it very strongly.

To a certain extent, you have to just try to live your life like it's normal, like you're healthy, and that you'll be healthy. I believe I'm healthier than I have been in years.

It's still mind over matter to a certain extent.

When my family first found out I was positive, I was not allowed to come home. They'd talk to me on the phone. Everything's all fine and dandy, but they'd find every excuse in the book for not to come home. Then my dad started reading; he educated himself to an extent. He lives in a dinky little town and they don't know nothing about nothing anyways. My brother and I used to be really close, but when he found out I was HIV positive, well, he has a new baby and he was afraid. He's very sheltered and very naïve and has a lot of misconceptions. His reaction is just to shut me out. We were always really close, and I just think he's scared that he's going to watch me be sick, and he's scared that he might get sick or the baby might get sick.

He just shut me out.

I'm really paranoid about getting sick. I try to do the best I can with my health, make sure I sleep every day, eat properly, and take my vitamins. Just little things, but they make a big difference. The food bank we go to, that one's really good; they give you a lot of fruit and vegetables, and you actually get quite a bit, which really helps make ends meet.

Some of the food banks were pretty gross (sighing), the food's all going bad. I mean you wouldn't want to eat it in the first place.

PWN will help you fill out your disability forms. I finally just did that last month. I was entitled to get this money years ago, but when you're busy doing drugs, who cares, right? In the last year or so, it's become common knowledge what you're allowed to have, and what you can get for extras. Most people didn't know that you can get extra money for this, or that there was a food bank here or a food bank there. It does make a big difference, especially for those people who are on meds because you absolutely have to eat. Some meds, you have to eat before you take them; sometimes, you have to eat after, but you can't just eat an apple, you have to have a full stomach. Being on welfare and trying to have a full stomach three times a day—good luck, right?

I've been so tired. I went and I got my blood work done yesterday, and then I went back to the doctor today. I'm just exhausted all the time now. I had massive trouble sleeping ... stressed out. The doctor put me on a non-narcotic sleeping pill, but I don't think it's strong enough.

Us people aren't allowed narcotics.

So I go buy my own off the street.

Valium really screws you up. I didn't know that it was that bad to get addicted to Valium. I decided to kick my heroin habit and my Valium habit at the same time. I thought, "Enough is enough!" I made it fourteen hours or something, and I was shaking uncontrollably. I phoned my mom, and I'm talking to her, and I'm crying and I'm, like, "I've never felt this sick." I can't stop shaking and I can't even get a glass to my mouth. I'd been eating handfuls of Valium for the last year. I didn't check out the withdrawal symptoms. I don't want to end up at that place again. It was really bad.

I'm using them *appropriately* now.

I don't do heroin much anymore because it takes so much to feel when you're on meth. I'm not on as high a dose as I should be, so I still get high if I don't take my meth. But what's the sense of getting into heroin when you're on methadone?

If you use a lot of heroin, you get constipated. I wouldn't go to the bathroom for, like, a week, and I'd have to literally make myself. From pushing and straining on my bowel, I got an abscess, and it swelled so much that it actually pushed on my appendix and my appendix was on the verge of rupturing so they took it out.

The very first time I ever had anything wrong from fixing, I was sharing a house with two other couples. While I was out, they let somebody into my room to fix. Well, I had a glass of water in there, and I guess they were cleaning their rigs and they had a glass of bleach. When I came home— well, it's my water (so I thought)—but I fixed bleach. I went to sleep and I was in so much pain that I woke up and thought my hand was broken, so I went to the hospital. They treated me like shit. They told me to quit whining and basically said that it was all my fault. I swear that doctor went out of his way to cause me pain. A lot of the hospitals, just because you're a drug addict, they won't give you anything when you're in pain. It doesn't matter if they can see that you're actually hurt. Your arm is broken and you know it hurts, but they won't give you anything.

I went to VGH a couple of years ago for surgery. I was there for three weeks and they were really good, they treated me like a human being. VGH has a rule: it doesn't matter who you are, a patient is a patient; if they say they're in pain then they're to be administered pain medication.

I had an abscess in my neck, both my ankles had abscesses, I had staph infection, I had cellulitis. I was there for two weeks on IV antibiotics, and I came out thinking, "This can't be it."

They were taking my blood every day to check my count, and my doctor was shaking his head, saying, "You know, you're really lucky with all the infection that your body has had to fight, that you actually have a good count. But it's not going to stay this way if you keep doing this."

I've always tried to use one fixing spot for a while so the other ones heal. I tried not to fix in my neck because it's a dangerous place to do it, but I did it on days when I was outside for long periods trying to make money. I was really, really cold and there wasn't anywhere else to fix, or I was so sick that my hands would shake so I couldn't do it and I had to get somebody to do it. I tried not to. Me personally, if I could get it into my body any other way I'd do it—if I could get the same effect. I hate using the needle.

The last time I did it, I got an infection and it went from there. It was from fixing, obviously, but it was what the dope was cut with that gave me the abscess, the crap that it was cut with.

Some people think that there's coke bugs in the coke. That started because there was a bad batch of dope that came in and it actually had parasites. What it did was, it made little brown blotches on your skin. It was easy enough to get rid of, you just had to wash with Selsin Blue® and it would take them away. But that started the whole thing, "There's bugs under my skin and you can see them moving." You know, people were convinced you could see them crawling right out of your skin, and so they'd pick, pick, pick, pick (*gesturing*). That was quite a few years ago, seven or eight. But there are bugs and bacteria. You don't know who's handled it before and coughed on it and sneezed on it, where it was cut up, whether dirty utensils were used or whatever. So there's lots of stuff in it and that's why you're supposed to filter it, but most people are in a hurry and they're in the back alley and they shake it, and away they go.

It used to be that you cut coke with certain stuff and you cut heroin with something else. But now people cut it with anything that will dissolve! The thing is, a lot of people, they don't know, they don't understand that some of these things you can't fix!

Just a couple of years back, they had people cutting coke with Ajax and Comet and people were croaking. Well, obviously! You just don't know now. You have no idea what you're getting now, none.

Most people smoke crack, it's already made and done. People cook it with ammonia—I don't care how small an amount of ammonia is in there, ammonia is a gas. When you cook it, it's corrosive and you're breathing that into your lungs. Crack's already bad for you! You're breathing that into your lungs, and you can't tell me that isn't eating away at your lungs! Some gives off a really strong gasoline taste or smell.

Now, people have a misconception—the bigger the better, right? So, the bigger the rocks, the better they think it is; but dealers are starting to cut it with things that expand. I think that people cut it with whatever they've got in their house that's free. See, a lot of these people are users and I can't see someone who's got a habit spending money.

When you first start doing dope you tend to be very, very mellow and very laid back about it. I could do a fix of coke, walk around for a little bit, lie down on my bed, and read a book. But now, people's tweaks get worse and worse. Some people start to get paranoid and think people are after them. I think that's a guilty conscience—people did-over other people, and now they're always worried someone's after their ass. I've never felt like that in my life.

I think tweaking's what your mind tells you when you're high.

Then there's the imaginary rocks—people actually get on their hands and knees and look around everywhere (*laughing*), wherever a rock may have dropped. I refuse to. They kick cigarette packages and they've got their sticks in the ground between the cracks in the cement, especially if they're convinced that the dealers have dropped their dope!

Then there's the "Hastings Shuffle" (*laughing*). You see people after they haven't slept for a couple of days, they're doing coke, they're bopping around, their arms are swinging, their legs are going, and they can't stand still when they're talking to you. That's the Hastings Shuffle. They're always in your face. It drives me nuts, man! Actually, they say that after you do coke—because it affects your nervous system—the longer you go, and the more you do, the less control you have over those muscles.

Since crack came around, people will do anything.

The other day we were talking about how things have changed so much over the years. Like, years ago, you saw young girls out on the street, you know, thirteen or fourteen, underage period. Whatever the age, you'd try to get them help and get them off the street. Now the dealers and the pimps, they see them out there and they hit them up!

"Come on! Here, let's get you off to work!"

To hell with getting them off the street. They just use them.

It's really sick.

With working girls, the standards and rules that they set for themselves—they're lost, they're gone. Before, it was almost like we had a union, there was a set price and they didn't go below that price. It was the only way to keep it on a roll. Now, the prices have fluctuated with the price of dope; dope goes down, the prices go down. A few years ago, there was a big drug bust so there was a lack of drugs and the price skyrocketed. You could always do a leeway—give somebody a break, a ten-dollar discount and that's it. If you were going any lower than that, then you were undercutting, you were going against the grain, and so you had to deal with everybody else. And you didn't want to deal with everybody else!

The guys knew that. They knew that they couldn't get it cheaper so they knew they had to pay the price. The thing is, would you rather do four dates or would you rather do one date? I would rather do one. Now, the girls don't even wait to see what these guys are going to offer them.

"Oh, oh, I'll give you a good deal," ten bucks or twenty bucks.

But they're cutting their own throat, and now these guys know they can get it cheap. Before it used to be mostly the older ladies who had trouble making money. It's worse working in the Downtown Eastside because people know and the dates know.

The girls go down the alley to do their dope, they come out and they'll be sitting there, not even paying attention to the drivers. They're on their knees scraping the ground for imaginary drugs and guys pick them up. God! Because they know that if they get her, it's going to be cheap—that they can take advantage of her because she's in a bad state.

And you still get these idiots that want to pay you more money or just figure the only way they'll take you out is to get you to agree to not use a condom. They think they can tell by looking at you that you're not sick. Well, you can't!

Their excuse is, "Well, I'm not sick. I'm married."

Well, big deal! Who'd your wife sleep with last week? Who'd you sleep with last week?

It's so stupid in this day and age, considering the amount of media attention and the information that's out there now. It wouldn't even cross a person's mind to not use a condom! I think they are just that uneducated; they're stupid. They live in their little houses on their little roads; they come down here and they figure that nothing applies to them because they're healthy and they've got a family and this and that. But you're never safer in one area than another.

Like, some people figure Granville Street's more high-class and you're safer; or on Victoria you're safer than on skid row. But, you know, the worst bad dates that I ever had weren't on skid row. They were in the so-called upper-class areas. So you're not safer anywhere else. You get the same lunatics wherever.

Sometimes you get people who just happen to want to do something good for the day. You see quite a few come down, and they'll park their vehicles and they'll just start giving away clothes and food and stuff like that. This one guy, I don't know when it was, but he won a bit of money—he wasn't a wealthy person—so he drove around on his bicycle and gave out twenty-dollar bills to girls. Just gave them out for nothing! He used to be a date, years ago. He used take me out and then he became an activist. He feels bad; he didn't intentionally set out to use or abuse anybody, but that's the way he sees what he did by taking out the girls. So he just goes around and he talks to them for a few minutes or so, asks if they want to go for coffee or whatever, and gives them ten or twenty bucks. It's just his way of trying to make it up.

It's not such a big necessity for me to go to work now because I'm on the methadone. It's not like I *have* to go work, at least I've got a choice now. Before, if the weather was bad, I would be, like, "Oh it's pissing rain or it's blizzarding out, oh well."

You've got to go. You don't have a choice.

Now, if it's a little bit chilly out, I don't want to go (*laughing*).

You can always tell the girls that are heroin addicts because, in the middle of winter, they're the ones that are out there in miniskirts and halter-tops. The cold almost doesn't bother you. That's the problem; you don't feel it—you're so doped up and you're out there in a miniskirt and a halter-top in freezing weather.

It'll make you sick.

In the summertime, the Union Gospel brings out juice because the girls will stand out there in the blistering heat and not drink anything. They get totally dehydrated. Unfortunately, you get into a bad pattern—if people won't bring it to you, you won't do it. If they don't bring you the food, you won't eat it. If I had to support my habit now, I'd be screwed. If I had to support a $200-a-day habit, I'd be out there all day and then I'd probably be sick half the time. It's ridiculous.

Quite a few years ago, I was out at work; it was really, really dead out and it was really cold—snowing—and of course I was out there in a miniskirt, in next to nothing. These two cops drove by me. I hadn't even really seen them around. They drove by at least three times, "Are you still here?"

I'm, like, "Yeah, I'm still here. No sense going home now, I'm going to make money sooner or later and I'm not going to make it inside my house."

They left, and half an hour or something later, they came back. I guess they had gone for dinner. They didn't bring me their leftovers; they actually brought me a steak dinner—baked potato and everything. They said, "Well, will you at least go home long enough to eat this and warm up?"

"Yeah, well, what do you want?" (*Laughing*)

"We don't want anything, we just want to see you go in long enough to eat this."

I thought that was pretty cool. I'm sure there are a couple of bad cops, but I don't believe it's as bad as they make it out to be.

Not so much now, but years ago, I heard that there were some cops that used to take advantage of the girls. But from my experience, I think that they weren't *real* cops. They were guys just pretending to be cops. Guys have picked me up and said, "I'm a cop and if you don't want to go to jail or whatever, then you'll do this or that."

I'd never been busted before, so I really didn't know what the routine was. You're afraid not to go through with it because, what if he was a real cop? Then you're even more afraid that he wasn't a real cop and that if you didn't go along with his game that he would get violent with you.

Over the years the cops have tried to "territory" us into a certain area so that we're easier to control. It's easier to keep an eye on people when they work in set patterns—here, at such and such a place on such and such a day, or whatever. You can notice if somebody is missing or if somebody's hurt, and it's easier to control the situation. They say, "You're not allowed to work, but if you're going to be in this area you must stay within these perimeters," which is just stupid.

They tried for a long, long time to get the girls to move even farther down by the bridge, to almost underneath the railroad tracks. It's not well lit and there's nothing around there, so if you scream nobody's going to hear you. It's deserted and the girls wouldn't go. Police were literally following you in their car at, like, two miles an hour, until you walked all the way down there. They wanted us to work underneath where it's industrial, where it's deserted and dark, and where nobody's around to say squat. They were harassing us so much, but I refused to go down there. Agencies made enough of a stink that they got off that trip, but they were really pushing it for a while.

There's always been problems up here with the residents complaining, to the point where they were out there pretending to be prostitutes. They get into these dates' cars and get them to drive around the corner into a bunch of picketers to humiliate them, which is the most dangerous thing somebody could ever do. I mean, the guy's going to go off the deep end, he's going to get scared or whatever, or mad, and knock her out. It's not as bad now, but the cops really laid it to the girls in the Mount Pleasant area. Picked you up, gave you area restrictions, and stuff like that.

The cops don't bother the girls so much anymore. Before, it was the girls that they preyed on, and now we're basically classified as the victims and they prey on the guys. Now the dates are more afraid to come down here, and you can't blame them. They're afraid it's going to become public knowledge, and that's what the cops always say, "I could write a letter to your work," or "I could show up at your work," or "I could write a letter to your wife." I don't know if I'd trust a cop again because they've done some nasty things. But now they have Dave Dickson.[18] He's really cool and, if anything, he's taught me to be more respectful of the police. I mean they've got their job to do, too. I can't hold that against them as long as they don't hold what I've got to do against me.

---

18. Dave Dickson is a well-respected and well-liked member of the Vancouver Police Department who has worked in the Downtown Eastside neighbourhood for many years.

They're a lot better now than they were a few years ago—the way they used to talk to us, like we were the scum of the earth. On a charge, they would basically tell me, "What the fuck do you want us to do about it? That's our job. If you don't want it to happen, don't do it."

"If I wasn't supporting my habit, I wouldn't do it."

I don't know, you can't really say they're not doing anything because you don't know, you're not there and you're not a cop, so you don't know what they're doing.

I carry mace. For a while I carried a knife, but the cops kept taking it away and I got really mad.

I'd say, "You're leaving me defenseless."

The last time a cop took it away, he said, "I'm not doing this to put you in a predicament, I'm doing this to save your life."

He says, "Look at you, you're in a vehicle with a guy who's got an adrenaline rush because he knows he's going to be violent with you. You're caught off guard, you pull the knife, and, no matter what, he's a man, you're a woman. What happens when he overpowers you and takes that and stabs you to death?"

It's true. I quit carrying one.

He says to use things like perfume or hair spray.

Girls lay charges against guys more often now because the cops are sympathetic and aren't abusive when you report things. They're on your side most of the time.

My preference is never to work in a vehicle because, even if you go to these scummy hotels here, you've got more of a fighting chance—you're not in a tiny little vehicle, not parked out in the middle of nowhere. Even in scummy hotels, somebody's liable to hear you; if you're locked in a vehicle, nobody's liable to hear you. Unfortunately, a lot of guys won't go to hotels and won't go to apartments because they've been ripped off, they've been set up before. I don't know, maybe it's being older and not using so much, but my head's a little clearer, and I think about things that normally wouldn't even cross my mind.

I had a really bad date a few years back and a buddy tried to kill me. I went back to work two days later. If that happened now, I don't know if I would be able to go back to work, if I would have the courage to go back on the street again. I heard about a girl who came in and said that a guy tried to lock her up and that there was no door handle on the inside of the vehicle. He had pit bulls in the back of his van. You hear a lot of that now, guys who've got their dogs with them in the vehicle.

I had another guy; just as soon as I asked him for the money up front, he started strangling me. I reported him. He didn't give me any bad vibes or anything. I didn't pick the spot and he didn't pick the spot, we kind of mutually picked the spot and it was right in the back of a residential neighbourhood, so I figured it was well lit and that it was okay. He even paid me, and everything. As soon as he paid me, as I turned my head to put the money away, he smashed me in the side of the head with a lead pipe that he got out of the trunk. He wanted me to lie down on the seat so he could tie my hands and legs behind me, but I kept struggling, "Let me go, I'm too tall, I can't lie down!" I kept trying to make excuses to get him to lay off.

It happened to this girl before me; he had actually tied her up and then changed his mind and decided to let her go. But she never reported it; it never even got brought up until before his trial. He actually just got out of jail a few months before that for raping women.

I've had three dates that were bad enough they had to be reported to the cops. Not that I had any faith they were going to do anything, but they were actually really good with me. They took me to a quiet spot and they gave me the benefit of the doubt. It wasn't, like, "Well, we're here to listen to you," but they basically told me—"We believe you, and if you help us, we'll do our best to help you back."

I believe one or more people are targeting women in the Downtown Eastside. A couple of these women on the missing women list I've known for many years. They weren't dope simple; they would turn people down if they had second thoughts. They had to have felt comfortable, and they would have been taken off guard because they just weren't dope simple, they wouldn't overlook things like the guy acting strange. Near the end, the girls that have gone missing were very street smart. What's worse is they have no idea; they've got no evidence. They've got nothing, and nothing to build on.

I did a TV interview with ——— on the missing women. They should've done a lot of things they didn't do. I wasn't very happy with it in the end. They cut out PHN,[19] and anything about PACE. They showed people full-face who had asked not to be shown, and they called them "ex-hookers."

---

19. PACE Health Network was a two-year, peer-driven project that provided health information and resources to people who work in the survival sex trade and who use drugs.

They even showed us in [another] piece on harm reduction, but I didn't want to be on TV. I'm the only one who voted no, because automatically people associate harm reduction with using.

I didn't want my son to see that on TV, and that's exactly what they did. What did they do before they showed us?

They showed skid row and people working and people dealing. So I thought that was really rude. In a way, they took something positive and made it negative.

I figure prostitution should be indoors and controlled so that people are sure to be healthy, that the guys know it's a set rule. It'll cut down on the violence. The government can get their money off it and it'll be off the street, unseen. You don't have to go to these places if you don't want to. People complain, "Well, I see hookers all over the place." Well, you know, you put us indoors and, if you don't want to see us, you don't go there, and that's your choice.

I was asked, "What's your ideal job?"

I got a job telephone soliciting—oh yeah, I just made a fortune! What a joke. But it was a legit job so that's all that counted, right? I don't know. Like, right now, I want to do something within PHN or PACE, but once I get some more education and I see what else is out there, then maybe something will click. PACE tries to find job alternatives for sex trade workers; they are there to help and they make no judgments. They at least try to give you alternatives. After working on the street for so long, you're really job-limited—not in your knowledge or anything, but in how you perceive authority.

I make odd money here and there—not much. I work one shift at ————, so I get ten bucks there, and then I work at a needle exchange office. It's just a small exchange and I give out condoms, needles, and stuff. It's for a non-profit agency, so every two weeks I get thirty bucks to go to our board meeting and every Tuesday I get thirteen bucks for working my Saturday shift. I always make a list of bills the day before welfare day. I go pay all that stuff first and see what I've got left. Then I go shopping and buy most of the stuff that I need for the whole month. I always give my friend some money to hang onto for me.

My friends say, "Hey, you eat so much chocolate cake you're sick of it. You can only eat so much chocolate cake before you get sick."

When you're with men twenty-four seven, you're working all the time and most of us have had bad experiences with relationships. Down here, what kind of relationship can you have? By the time you get home the last thing you want to see is another dick. I've got nothing against men and I'm attracted to them—I'm attracted to women, too. Personally, I'd rather be with a man, but it's too hard because I'm working and it always seems to screw up. Women understand more because they're usually doing the same thing. It's complicated. For me, it just comes down to need fulfilling; it's not even sexual. A lot of the girls have had such bad relationships and gone through so much bullshit with men that enough is enough. I don't think it's a defense mechanism, but they end up turning to women, not because they're more sexually drawn to women, but just because they couldn't have men anymore. It was just that there was so much bullshit that went along with it, that it was a do or die situation. I find that after they stop working they usually—not all, but most—go back to a male/female relationship.

I go for coffee with this one guy. He reads, and we basically have the same taste in books. Once in a while he'll get spy novels, and I don't really like those. We trade books back and forth, and then when we're both done he takes them back to his buddy at the bookstore and trades them in for another few books.

Sara (as she finishes reading the final edit of her story): *Seems a funny place to end.*

Leslie: *Yeah, would you like to add anything now? Write a different ending?*

Sara (after a pause): *No. This is fine.*

Leslie: Why do you want to publish your story?

Sara: I have a whole bunch of reasons for publishing this. For once, I get to say my piece. I've done a lot of interviews on this and that around my life, around things from downtown like the missing women. A lot of stuff that I said was taken out of context or wasn't portrayed properly, and in the end it looked like non-truths. So this is finally my chance to say something and for it to be accurate. If it helps people who are in my situation, or who have somebody in my situation, or if it just helps them to understand a little better about people in general, without misconceptions and stereotypes, then I've accomplished something.

But my main thing is if it's going to be said, it's going to be true.

You were saying a minute ago, that when you originally did these interviews, things were quite different for you.

Yeah, I wasn't in a good place in my life then. I was angry with a lot of things, and, even though the stuff that I said was all true, there are times when you are in that kind of space and you have tunnel vision, you can only see one way. I said certain things about my family and my partner and whatever else I happened to have not been too happy about (*laughing*).

Things have really changed and, at that time, things were starting to change. My priorities were starting to change, and that had a lot to do with where I was. It was a big struggle for me. I wanted to get my life on a better track. Where my heart said one thing, my body kept doing the other. It was really hard for me, and I was really angry, not just with myself, but with everybody.

Now I'm at a place where I'm a little better. I've started getting things together. I've still got a long way to go, but now I'm pregnant and I'm going to have a baby soon. That changes your life immensely. Even before I got pregnant, I was trying to cut down on my dope and trying to see things in a better light and get more involved in my community. At the beginning, I was starting to do stuff with PACE, and I got more involved with them and other places as well. I don't know, the terminology is stupid, but it's true; I feel more self-worth.

I'm just in a better place and my family's in a better place, my partner's in a better place. I'm not working anymore and I'm more involved with my family. I went to see my dad for the weekend, and he was genuinely happy to see me. We went out for dinner and his wife had bought me baby stuff. They're both just as excited about having a grandchild as I am. We're starting to pull together a lot more.

When I first started doing the interviews, that's when I was struggling to begin trying to start my life anew. I'm still struggling. But I'm a hell of a lot further than I was at the beginning.

Before I got pregnant, I saw people on the street eight months pregnant, smoking crack, and I was really judgmental. I said some nasty things to people. I tell you, it's sure a lot different when you're in that place. It's easy to say, harder to do; your mind can play some nasty games with you.

Drugs are the stem, not the root of my problems, but that's how I dealt with them. I'm learning to deal with them without doing the drugs, and that's the hard part because you get in such a rut for so many years doing the same thing. Even though you're not happy there, you keep yourself there. It's dumb but it's true. That's my biggest struggle. I'm also trying to get into a more stable life, not working, which is hard for me too. Not because I want to go to work—that's the last thing that I want to do—but money gets tight, and your first thought is, well, I can go to work. So far so good. The longer I don't do it, the harder it is for me to go back out.

What do you want people to get from hearing your story?

I want to say, keep plugging away. It will come! It will.

But the thing is, it will come when you are ready for it to come, and it won't come any sooner, it won't come any later. I say it doesn't matter how much you want it, if it's not time, it's not going to come. I tried over and over and over and over and always fell flat on my face. But you just have to pick yourself up and try it again because, if you're stubborn enough, sooner or later it's going to work. You have to be ready, and even though I was trying to do what I wanted at the time—and I thought my heart was in it—I wasn't totally there, so it didn't work.

Don't give up.

Six

DEE

EDITORS' INTRODUCTION

Beginning in the early 1990s, neighbourhood women in the Downtown Eastside began organizing what has become an annual event: the Valentine's Day March against Violence and Poverty. In recent years, the Missing and Murdered Women have been the focus of this demonstration. The march begins at the Carnegie Centre on Main and Hastings and winds its way down Hastings Street, detouring through alleys and parks. Adopting a tactic made famous by the Madres of the Plaza dey Mayo in Argentina, many carry pictures of their missing relatives. Women stop to smudge[20] outside notorious bars, strip clubs, in alleyways, in parking lots, and beside dumpsters where women's bodies have been found. They read the names of women who have died, tell how they died, and list their relations: mother of ———, sister of ———, daughter of ———, friend of ———. In this way they "inscribe" these women's lives on land, and in place.

It is appropriate that there is so much focus on mourning and death. Perpetual, repetitive, relentless experiences of tragic loss permeate the lives of individuals and families in this community. In the case of the Missing and Murdered Women, the strongest criticism of the police—and by proxy, of the public—is that early reports were ignored because the women were "prostitutes," "addicts," Aboriginal, invisible. In their struggle, visibility and recognition are inseparable from the goals of material survival; these women are engaged in an effort to stay alive and to change the material and symbolic conditions of existence for women who come after them.

In "Fears," Dee's description of street life tells of the frequency and degree of violence endured by women who work the street-level sex trade. Their visibility within the community sometimes dissuades women from reporting violent incidents, as they are vulnerable to recriminations—both from the legal system and from their attackers.

Dee speaks about days of heavy drug use and of her spiritual and physical struggles along the road to recovery. She marks milestones that may appear insignificant to those unfamiliar with that goal. Given the close relationship between drug use and sex work for many women, *not* working the street and *not*

---

20. Smudging is a ritual of blessing and purification performed by Aboriginal peoples where the smoke from burning sweet-grass or sage is drawn towards the head and body in a gesture of cleansing.

using daily represent substantial strides. Recovery is a difficult internal process that includes coming to terms with the past and finding your way through a variety of treatment regimens that may, or may not, be individually meaningful.

Fears

Edited from interviews conducted August 2001–March 2002
Interviewer: Leslie A. Robertson

Being an Aboriginal woman, a street person, and a drug user, I have a lot of fears based on what revolves around my addiction.

I have to solicit to provide for my habit.

A week ago there was another Native girl found behind the Astoria Hotel, and it's really affected me to the point where I don't want to have to go and risk my life for my next drug use. It's kind of intimidating me into wanting recovery a little more. I'm sober more than I'm high now. I'm not sure if that has to do with my health condition or all the women that are disappearing. Either way, you've got to come to reality, to know that you're self-destructing.

It's quite intimidating.

I grew up on the reservation. I'm Salish, Native Indian. I first moved to Vancouver when my mom lost her job and she moved to educate herself in computers and stuff like that. I was fourteen going on to fifteen, totally uprooted from my high school, you know, not knowing anybody. Still, I did really well in school; like, academically, I was right up there. I got good grades, was passing everything.

I lived with my sisters [when] I was going to school.

Didn't graduate though, I got pregnant in Grade 11.

When I got pregnant, I lived with a roommate and then, from there, went from roommate to roommate to roommate (*laughing*).

I never really had a stable home or lived anywhere for more than six months.

My first drug of choice was always marijuana.

When I was first introduced to crack it was just a social thing. I didn't really get hooked on it the first few times.

I was introduced to coke and prostitution by my first boyfriend—like real, intimate boyfriend. It was really bizarre; he introduced me to the drugs and I didn't think a whole lot of it at first. I watched him and I just smoked marijuana. It turned from bad to cruel; watching it was bad, and then, after a while, he'd get abusive, he'd get a mean streak in him. I guess it was just a defensive thing on his part ...

He'd take it out on me because I wasn't using the stuff at that time. This was crack. He was a number of years older than me and I'd never turned a trick or anything before that, never really had a real sexual relationship. I was really naïve to have fallen for an abusive guy because I'd never experienced ... I don't know, the sex thing, anyway. I know it had to do with that because I was so inexperienced, and he obviously gave me the attention I needed.

I was with him for nine months before I actually did crack for the first time—like, in a way that I'd like to keep on doing it. He gave me more so that I needed it, wanted it and needed it. So, you know, it gave him control at the same time, and that was a real downfall for me.

Today, I see [that] as being somewhat of a coke slut or being simple so you can have the dope—doing what's asked of you so that you can have your next fix or whatever. It's a little far-fetched for me right now because I wouldn't do it (*laughing*). I'm a little older and a little more experienced. There's so much I wouldn't do now (*laughing*), that I did with him.

It was the sex, the drugs, the money, and the power!

I couldn't see it then, but my eyes are wide open to it now because I see it on the street and the girls are so young and they're so stupid! (*Laughing*) Just like I was!

It has to do with the drug, the manipulation; the power to give you the next fix—and wanting the next fix! They use money, clothes, fashion, or style. I remember he did my hair and he bought me roses and stuff like that. It was like everything a woman wants—apart from the abuse. But this money trip is an ongoing thing, so it was all a money-ego trip as far as I saw it. When I see it now, it's, like, rich people suck because of how they treat the lower class.

Anyways, he got me hooked and I was constantly told to fill his every desire. That went on for years; so did the abuse.

My poor boy, he really suffered due to the using.

Yeah, it's really sad that the ones we love have to suffer!

I finally did leave ———. Actually, I went back to the rez to get away from him and he never came up there. I go to the rez to clean up, but I relapsed again. They say there's no dope there but you've got to be awful rich;

everything's twice as much there as it is here, so getting it is a little more difficult.

Anyway, so I came back. I'm working the streets and my very first bad trick is some guy that just got me to do him and didn't pay me. I guess that would be my first bad experience working the street. I was living in social housing. My son was just a little boy, like three or four, and I'd leave him with a baby-sitter and go work the streets. The baby-sitter would be from the Ministry, and I guess they put a tail on me and found out what I was doing while he was in their care. They apprehended him on those grounds—that I was putting him at risk of being around these guys. I never took the dates home.

So, yeah, that would be when my son got apprehended and put into the system, which is where he is now. I wasn't full-blown using. I'd go on an outing every second week when I could get my own baby-sitter, you know, thinking that I'm fooling the Ministry and I was only fooling myself (*sighing*).

So my son went into the system and they clue into what I'm doing—the housing. I lose that apartment and that was low rental. I lost my apartment over prostitution. I didn't get charged or anything, but from then on, I just lived from crack shack to crack shack because my son wasn't there and I didn't have any responsibility.

Crack shacks are full of users; they're using spaces and if you do crash there you're an insider and you know the people really well. All I had were my clothes, which I left at Mom and Dad's. I went to change whenever I thought enough of myself to want to change my clothes and have a shower; brush my teeth. I mean you just don't do that stuff when you're on drugs! It's just disgustingly dirty, and, when I'm sober, that's how I feel—dirty.

I'm constantly brushing my teeth and showering, bathing.

So, I'm working the street.

I'm working the streets at this time, and I run into this guy. He's got money, lots of money, and it turns out that he really likes me. After he's picked me up on the street a couple of times, he starts to come and see me every day! So I start making him pay for my time. He likes me so much; he can pay for my time. Every day I had money to use—that's always in the back of every addict's head, you know, the next fix or whatever, the next rock. So he starts seeing me every day, for, like, three months—daily, if not every other day. I figure this guy likes me and I'm starting to like him. He's spending a lot of money and taking me places, so he asks me if I'll spend a couple of days at his place. I say, "Well, sure," and he says he'll buy me drugs, and he does.

So we end up living together for four years. Throughout that time, he's supporting my habit and he has life savings, he has stocks and bonds and investments and RRSPs—and he's a trick!

Every time he scored me mass amounts of drugs, I'd have to do whatever with my body, whatever he wanted. I stayed in that relationship and then we had a child. I worked at ———, on the cleaning crew then. So, we have our child and I can't stop using. I end up having a crack baby, and he supports my habit throughout the pregnancy. After the pregnancy, he doesn't want me using, he wants me taking care of the baby. So I, da da da da da ...

I clean up, I take care of the family, and I do the cooking.

That's always short-lived because we're addicts, and even though we're clean for two years, our minds are still conniving and we're only kidding ourselves. I'd sneak the odd one in while he was at work, he'd come home and he'd take one look at me and he'd know. Like, you know, baby's just a year and a half, two years old, she's running around the house and I'm smoking rock! Anyways, that's also short-lived. She's apprehended and we go through a separation and he tells me I have to clean up or he's going to take the baby and leave me.

I go into a recovery house and he comes to see me every weekend. I do a treatment program only to use not even a week after I get out. I remember that so well, four days out of the treatment centre and I go back out to use. But, you know, I remember feeling forced into programs so that I could keep my family. The way I felt in the programs, I felt like I was doing time in jail or something.

So anyways, he gives me a chance, and this is when I go back home and this is my best clean time—three years. I pack up all my stuff and I go back to the rez. I did a river bath every morning when I got up. You go into the water and under the water to pray to the Creator for something you need within yourself, like courage to face another day, or guidance, or hope.

Now, this is where the molestation comes in, because I see the guy. I have a flashback and I tell my whole family about it for the first time. It took twenty years for me to open that can of worms.

I got pregnant again—this is when we're seeing each other on weekends and going out to see the baby in foster care. My parents are doing the daycare and he gets custody of our child. So, he's coming up every other weekend on paydays, but little do I know that, while I'm there, cleaning up, pregnant, and taking care of my other two kids, he's down here and he's having an affair!

I find that out when I'm seven months pregnant, and I'm BIG pregnant.

The baby was nine pounds eight ounces. She was too big. I couldn't push her out; they had to use the suction to pull her out. I relapsed after I had her. I heard what he's doing and he's been seen in public with this woman.

So I relapse and he gets custody—this is after three years clean.

"Everything is gone and will never return," was my attitude.

Life became worthless.

I came back here after my relapse—you know, back to the source of making money. So anyways, he's with her, they move in together, and I'm on the street. I'm homeless and I'm using pretty chronically. I had never injected before. I started injecting when he started seeing someone else.

I've lived in the Downtown Eastside for four years.

When I first came, I was homeless. I didn't start injecting on the reserve; I started with a guy that I really, really liked. He's dead now, I couldn't save him. I didn't know how to do CPR.

All I did was use, work on the streets, and sleep, that's pretty much what my routine was. When I was making the most money, by the end of the weekend I'd have no money, no food, sometimes, no place to stay. You know, it's crazy where addiction will bring you and where you'll allow it to take you.

Down here, I moved from hotel to hotel, or we got evicted from apartment after apartment. I lived in three hotels here.

They're all shooting galleries of some kind, where there's drugs and drug users around to either support or have them support you. So they were selected just to keep me in the environment of using and having access to using. Another one of the situations that is real bad is hanging out at the shooting galleries or the gathering places where the addicts score and do their dope. Then you have the overdoses. It's just the viciousness of the lifestyle, you know. The bottom line is there's no friends when drugs are concerned.

I'm a loner now.

The next step, you go from crack shack using into isolation, where you use alone and you can't share or you get too fucking weird when you do use. I guess it's about paranoia, you know, "Look at where I've been and I have every reason not to trust anybody!"

I have gone through not sleeping for almost a couple of weeks at a time. It's incredible that the body can stay up that long if you have the drugs to ingest constantly. Otherwise, you do fall on your face, hallucinations big time! I remember smoking crack and hiding under the bed thinking that there's somebody actually hiding around there.

Oh, paranoia big time!

When you're using for that long, being up that long, and then tripping that way—on the street we call that tripping red. When you're tripping red, you die! Tripping red's real scary; I've done it a few times! It's when you're doing too much, when it starts doing you, instead of you doing the drug!

I'll tell you one of my incidents.

I was IV using at the time. This isn't crack using; this is injecting coke in a stairwell, down the street from the crack house, because I'm too wigged out to fix in front of anybody. I'm a closet case at this time. So I do this injection and I'm in a stairwell and there's a window there. Okay, first the walls turn red and then the sky turns a lighter touch of red, like blood. Then it all starts running down the walls. I get up and I run out of that place! And at the same time I was hearing "Amazing Grace."

I'm running down the alley from what? From my own imagination.

That's just the extreme. It's really scary.

That's my own experience.

I'm telling you, I was so fucked up when I was injecting and smoking. Even sometimes now, if I stay up too long, I'll hear things, hallucinate that way. I'd hear my kids crying. I have three kids, and I'd hear all three of them at different times.

I come down hard on myself about what kind of mother I am; what kind of person I am. You know, is God going to forgive me if my kids are getting hurt while I'm out doing all this shit?

I think it is a sign and I think there is a guardian angel that puts that sign there. I believe in heaven and I believe in God and I believe in spirits—good spirits and bad spirits.

I'm going to tell you another incident of spirits.

I was injecting, and this place was a drug-infested place prior to when I moved in there. It probably still is a drug-infested place. I guess a lot of people have died there, either violently or drug overdoses. Anyways, I was injecting at the time, and I'd had a few experiences with spirits while I was living in this certain apartment building. This one time I opened the balcony door and it went right through me. It scared me; it was a bad spirit!

I've never asked them what they want. Someone told me to ask them.

I'm wearing a crucifix now so I haven't been seeing them and I haven't been sensing them.

One time, I was injecting and as I was injecting it was halfway through the rig and these three come right through the wall and they say, "Come with us." I pulled the thing right out of my arm! I think I would have died. I think that was a sign that I was going to kill myself. At that time, my partner was in jail and it was Christmas time and I was being really hard on myself! I was intentionally doing too much. You know I'm a closet case user; I'm by myself. I could die at any time and nobody would find me.

So at that time I'm injecting in every alley and any alley.

It's creepy once you start.

I started out with coke. What I think is, they gradually put a little heroin in every time so you become more dependent. I eventually had a heart attack and I ended up in St. Paul's Hospital, in cardiac with a bunch of senior citizens! I was the youngest person in the whole ward. That was ten years ago, and I was twenty-two. Even after that, as soon as I was conscious and I was able to walk around in the hospital, I disconnected myself from the IV and all the monitors they had on me. I took it off to go and fix again. After that, I would binge use with the IV. I smoked crack at that time too. Then I'd end up back in the hospital. I did that for a few years until I met my partner.

So anyways, those were injecting days, when I was in self-destruct.

My boyfriend helped me by showing me he cared.

I was able to stop injecting.

He OD'd in front of me. We were at the crack shack and he was drinking; I'm in the other room and he's up and around, he's socializing, he's drinking moonshine and he's really, really loaded. And then I don't hear him, and I know that there's heroin in the house, and I get up and I go into the kitchen.

This is the one that I save.

I performed CPR and I had to do his breathing until the paramedics came because he was right under. You have to breathe for him until the ambulance comes. I'm still seeing him; it's going on six years.

It was a year and a half after my separation from my marriage. He didn't want someone who was using needles. To get off it wasn't so bad because I was falling in love with this guy. I was just able to stop. I didn't have to go to detox or something. I just liked him enough to not want to do it.

NA has never worked for me. I don't know, maybe I have a problem with how the people hang on to their old ways. You know, street rules and street ways and the street talk, the toughness, the ego, and everything.

With traditional, it's all or nothing. With traditional, you've got to go with the Creator's guidance or you ain't cutting it, you're still on the Black Road. They call it the Red Road when you follow the Creator. The Creator's will for you is the Red Road and the Black Road is to stray from his guidance.

Right now, I'm kind of sitting on the fence with wanting recovery and still having access to my addiction. I use once or twice a week, I'm not totally clean. I still use and I still have access to using because of my regulars.

Almost five years since I [stopped] IV use I started up again. My doctor was really upset but happy that I was able to be honest, to tell him why I had to go in to see him. I was having a hard time breathing, and my fingers are still numb from irregular heartbeat. I was having heart murmurs from injecting. I'll do it once a week or once every other week. At first I was justifying it, "It's okay, I'm not doing it when my boyfriend's around, I'll be okay. I'll be safe using IV." We live separately now, so there's times when we're not together and I will have the drug.

Being open and talking honestly, it's a real scary reality. We all die out here using unless we come to grips with our own realities, accept who we are and where we've been in our lives, which is recovery, right? The basis, I think, of recovery is self-acceptance, and right now, it's a real hard thing for me. I just want to talk mostly about what's been my incentive to clean up—or attempt to.

I'm not clean yet but I don't work the streets very much anymore. My reason for not wanting to work on the street is that there's a serial killer that's killing the sex trade workers. They're missing and their bodies are never recovered. So that's my incentive to stay clean.

Right now, I'm stuck thinking that men are just money to me, and to turn another trick is just to use more. I was run by a pimp about five years ago, and I actually went into a transition house at that time to get away from this guy because he was running our lives. We were working for him, you know, we had all the nice clothes and everything. When it came right down to it, none of it matters. Your safety matters first, and when it turns to abuse and trauma—what you'll put up with so that you can have your next fix! It's really not worth it! Back then I didn't have as clear a mind as I do now.

Yeah, I endured a lot of physical abuse, almost like torture. Fucking hard lesson, letting a man run your life for you; telling you when you eat, when you sleep, when you work, and when you get your next fix.

Being a prostitute and having to support your habit, where do you draw the line? It's the money! The money's fast. There was a time when I'd make a thousand dollars on the weekend and I'd have no money left, I'd have no food, nothing. I'd be going to food line-ups.

I am letting go of the prostitution, I'm just too afraid out there. It's really freaked me out that girls are still going missing. Out of all the women that are missing they don't find most of them. It's pretty awful when you're shaking or you're trembling because you don't know, "Is this guy going to be the one that kills you?"

It's gone from bad to worse. I had two black eyes last month from a broken nose, a bad date. Yeah, and that one I got out of! He tried to rape me; he had no money. I sat on the horn. That horn has saved me more than once!

I have had three bad dates that I can remember distinctly. I was raped and strangled by a guy. I was starting to pass out as he was strangling me and then he let me go. It was wintertime about four years ago. We had had a really frigid spell that time and he drove away. I had to run down the street with just my jacket on—no pants, no shoes, nothing. Two weeks later, this guy tried to pick me up again and I turned him in. I got scared and I never showed up in court. I was afraid that he'd hurt me before court.

I did have another bad date a year ago, and this guy knocked out four of my teeth. Well, he broke one and he knocked three of them right out, but they're broken under the gums so I had to have surgery. It took eight needles and a surgical procedure to remove the tooth. I still have to go back two more times. To top it off, I had students working on me; digging that needle around in my gums! They had to get the dentist in to find the nerve after three or four tries, and those needles are big!

You know, basically, I'm afraid, and there's a lot of paranoia, but once you're traumatized, it never leaves.

So all my highs are very fearful, fear-based.

I got five grand when I got strangled and I ended up giving my thirteen-year-old fifteen hundred to go spend. I didn't give it to him flat out all at once. I gave him three or four hundred at a time and told him, "Bring me back receipts, make sure it's all accounted for." He did really well. I was impressed. He got his room set up.

He's got everything any boy could want—except his mom. I'm sorry, but he still has my heart.

I think I'll put this in the story because it's part of it. My boy is an alcoholic, and he's fallen into the pattern of addiction. It's up to him to break the chain now; it isn't up to me. His addiction has caused severe consequences at an early age. A part of me wants to blame myself, because I wasn't a stable enough parent for my own child.

My son fell into addiction because of my pattern of addiction. I know that's how it works. A child will only learn what he's taught.

I'm grateful to my parents that they have a stable home; that they have good lives going for themselves. My mother is a good provider for my son. I'm missing out on his adolescent years, his voice squeaking and changing. I've only heard it on the phone.

My other kids are wards of the province, and it's almost like they're not even my kids anymore. I wasn't seeing them when I was using. What I really, really, really have missed out on is my girls.

I have one crack baby. She doesn't need any therapy or methadone; she went through some withdrawal at birth. It's really, really difficult because they have a hard time nurturing and feeding, so the bond is a little more difficult because they cry more. When I was pregnant with her, I smoked a lot of crack and I couldn't stop. After the fifth month my doctor just said, "Well, you've got to use until the end now because the withdrawal will be too much for the child."

Withdrawal when I was pregnant.

I found that was kind of strange that I was encouraged to continue to use when I was pregnant, but she wasn't given any methadone or anything. They just kept her under observation and helped me learn how to feed her, bottle-feed her. I couldn't nurse because I was using. She doesn't need therapy, she's doing really well in school and she's a normal kid in every sense. I need to be thankful for that. I was really hard on myself being a mother to her.

My other daughter was not even six months old when I left, and she's almost six years old now. I can't have any more kids. She was big; she was nine pounds, eight ounces (*laughing*). I couldn't have any more after that.

I haven't seen my girls in a couple of months now. I only see them three or four times a year. It's hard as a mother and an addict, you know, to hope for recovery. There was never enough clean days. I couldn't go out of my way to see them because I couldn't put the dope down long enough to realize how much I need them rather than them needing me. It's like I'm missing out in a bad way!

Yeah, I had beautiful girls.

Talking makes me feel better inside; it's really kind of strange. It's therapeutic in the sense that we're talking about our past addictions. It's coming out, and we're realizing the destruction. I guess we're recognizing that, [with] abstinence, life got good for a time. There was improvement in the value of life and an appreciation of who you really are. What I really miss is being a mom—you know, the responsibility, and being looked-up to and the respect by the kids.

I'm really working on coming to grips with my life, what I've done to it. Every time I've cleaned up, my clean time has been longer. I did have two years and then I had three. I'm looking into hopefully getting out of it before disappearing. It's given me the incentive to not work the streets. I've gone out maybe a dozen times in the last three or four months, which is really minor for me, and that's minimized my using.

It's kind of intimidating being a Native woman and being a prostitute and a drug user. The majority of the victims are Native women, and it's really scary that I might die if I continue to stay out there. It's really freaked me out that girls are still going missing. I have nightmares. A Native woman and a white lady went missing last month, and their bodies haven't been recovered.

All I know is, there's almost fifty women who are babies of some mother, and that's the bottom line.

Last weekend there was a *Vancouver Sun* dude cruising around the streets, and he was talking to each of us, showing us a picture of the latest eighteen-year-old that went missing! It's keeping me from working the street because I'm afraid to be one of those pictures. Just to think that it could be me.

When I had cravings bad enough, I had someone taking plate numbers for me because I was afraid out there.

I've been in and out of addiction for the last fifteen years, since I gave birth to my first child. I'm thirty-two now. I can't say how it is for other people, but there was a lot of pain for me, and it covered it up. My using hides my fears, my aches and pains, and it doesn't justify anything. It is a temporary mask to wear.

From IV using, I contracted hepatitis C, which is damaging my liver, and that's a progressive illness as well. As long as you use and inject more drugs, it damages your liver. I feel it when I eat, after I eat, it affects my digestion because I fall asleep. I get really tired, low energy.

There's nights where I cry because I want the drug. I taste the drug. I feel like I'm under the influence of the drug when I wake up from a dream. It's one of the worst feelings I think that I've ever experienced, this craving for the substance I'm dependent on.

I dream about being high and I think I'm high when I wake up.

I find that I'm substituting addictions. I'm not using daily; I use, say, on Saturday night, all night Saturday, which means that I go through the withdrawal right after that. I'm just getting through the withdrawal stages and then I get the cravings and I use again, which means that I start withdrawal all over again.

It's edgy. I'm all over; I'm tapping my foot and whatever. I won't sleep, I won't keep still, and I'll be really moody. Oh, boy, can I be a real witch! I'll phone home, I'll cry to my mom, and she'll send money because she knows that I'm unstable. I can't cope and I have resorted to crime in the past.

I never wanted to hurt people, I just want money, but whether they get hurt or not doesn't matter at the time. I've been convicted of robbery and I'm not proud of it. I caused bodily harm to an elderly woman and it's one of the worst things in my life that I think has happened! They wanted to give me five years in prison for it and instead they gave me a five-year conditional sentence. I'm serving my sentence in the community and keeping the peace and maintaining good behaviour. So far so good!

I was an IV user at the time, and my behaviour was ... I couldn't control myself. I did that for thirty bucks! I'm really sorry that I did her harm. If she'd broken a bone she'd have never recovered. She was old and I was mean to do that. That's about the dumbest thing I've done for drugs!

It seems like the street life has created problem after problem for me, and it's never-ending. Every problem seems worse than the last one—the seriousness of it.

The fear for me is, is the result going to be death, regardless if it's addiction or working the street ...

Having periods of being sober gives me insight into reality (laughing). If you want to call it that!

When I'm straight, I feel like I'm dirty; I bath a lot, I shower four or five times a day. It's gross that so many guys have touched me and that I've slept with so many men. I feel dirty.

Today, at least, I know there's another existence besides being afraid. There's no real pleasure in using for me anymore. Basically, I need to learn different things, to live in a different way. It's like what we see is what we learn, and as long as we subject ourselves to the same thing over and over, then we don't learn much more than that. Addiction is like a circle; we just keep going around in a circle—turn the trick, to buy the dope, to use, and then turn the next trick, to buy more dope, to use more. Working and using are totally linked. It's a cycle.

I'm not an everyday user anymore; when it's accessible, that's fine by me. I get up at nine o'clock, ten at the latest. I don't get up and head out to "ho" kind of thing (laughing). You know, I don't live to use, my every waking moment isn't based on my next high. It was only a couple of months ago, before all these girls started disappearing. I don't have to be out on the streets anymore now that I've got a new place. I have regular tricks that I've known over the years that have my phone number and come to my house. I live there by myself.

I got a job six weeks ago ... I prepare meals for street people. I've been focusing everything in my life around that little two days of work. I'm clean the day before I go to work. I use on payday. That's a big step from living from one fix to another—to using once a week. So my life has gone from the street and being a crack user to being productive (*laughing*).

I still feel like I'm where I'll always be, and will I die here or what? But I feel like I'm safe, I know I'm safe where I live.

I think it's a good thing that they have security here. I'm not working around the clock, twenty-four hours a day, seven days a week, so it doesn't really affect my day-to-day living, whereas other girls that are still in addiction are quite upset about the security—the no visitors at night. I don't have a problem with it. It seems like a safe thing for their lifestyle anyway, considering the things that can happen, the risks that you're taking. The staff is really decent about being there for you; they're so supportive if I need anything resource-wise. They go out of their way to send me to a counselling session or they get a reference and they set me up with someone.

I have problems reaching out.

I know there's lots of resources around, but there hasn't been a real connection with my counselling, so I'm bouncing all over the place. I don't feel like my therapy is rooted, that I'm standing on two feet or solid with the direction that I need to go. I have a hard time trusting people.

With our culture, as a Native person, we have security around our own kind of people. We have a lot more trust in our own people than we would in, say, society's majority. Finding the right alcohol and drug counsellor is the most beneficial part of my getting better. My biggest issue is my childhood trauma.

A lot of my growing years, and still today, I have a fear of men. It's really weird that I'd have that kind of job, you know—prostitution. I guess, in a sense, I learned that it does things for me. It gets me things—what I want—so it's kind of an easy thing to back into.

You know, I used to train. I used to be a runner, I used to do track and field; I was very athletic. I loved who I was back then and I hope that someday I can train again. Right now, all I can do is the stretches because of my heart condition and because I was just hit by a car.

I was at Main and Hastings, I had one foot on the curb and one on the street, I flew twelve feet and I have no feeling in one leg where it impacted.

There's still a lump there. That was really painful and that guy really hurt me. In his report to the police he said he accidentally stepped on the gas instead of the brake. He could have killed me!

I've gained fourteen pounds. I think it's because I'm not on the street, it's kind of levelling me out in more ways than one, like, mentally, physically, and spiritually. I'm more in tune with myself. I think more when I'm clean and I'm trying hard. I can think positively. My new year's resolution is to get a job; my incentive is to sober up. I'm more than proud to do this publication.

My perfect future is to get recovery and be okay with who I am. My main concern right now is mental. I've had a nervous breakdown. I was in an "I-love-me jacket" (*laughing*) because they thought I was going to hurt myself. I totally went off the deep end. I drank hard stuff, I was on anti-depressants, and I hadn't taken them for a few days so I was kind of reacting to the withdrawal. I went to the hospital.

I don't even want to remember it. My family wouldn't come. They thought it was a crank call and they wouldn't come and get me out of the nut house!

I have relatives in the city. I talk to them and I hear the same thing from them. "Just get off the shit." It's easier said than done. I'm trying. I'm trying really hard, but I'm not doing it yet.

I need three weeks clean to go into treatment, and I haven't accomplished that yet. My max is one week, and then I just fall off. I'm on a couple of wait lists for recovery houses, and they're six months long (*laughing*). I want to go to a government-funded one. I don't want to just go to any quick gig—one where someone's going to run off with the money.

I have a clothing allowance of seventy-five dollars because I'm cleaning up. I'm starting to buy my own food. I spend about twenty dollars a week on food only because I want to be home and out of the street scene. I eat four to five times a day, little pieces here and there; I'm not gorging myself on full meals.

I really want to stay away from the food lines, that way you stay away from the users. I'm learning the hard way. I go to the food banks, I won't go to the free food lines because—even some of the support groups I've been going to—it's okay for them to have people there when they're high. I can't go for that reason. I can't be around people when they're high because it triggers a craving.

My health is good right now; I'm not going to say excellent.

I wear a jacket that I used to wear when I made the track and field team, so it's an incentive for me to have that on. There was a time in my life when I had a lot of pride in who I am, and I'm hoping to maybe find half of that someday.

Dee added the following written addendum in May 2003.

My life has improved an extreme amount. In September 2002 I stopped using prescription drugs and have come out of a life of believing I was not worthy. It's been eight months since I took a pill because I didn't like myself. I remember I'd take three pills if I didn't like how I looked in the mirror. Or, if my boyfriend was drinking, I'd take five pills and sleep the entire weekend. I couldn't be put down or cursed if I wasn't awake. My pill addiction wasn't known to many people. I bought most of them or traded 'em with neighbours. I wonder at times, where the strength and courage not to use pills anymore went, because today I am still beaten by my crack addiction. One to two times per week I use crack. It isn't what it once was. I once lived to smoke rock every day.

I have endured bad things because of smoking rock. But most of all, being a prostitute destroyed me, not only because [it] got me the money to use. When I cleaned up, got my children, and moved to the rez, at least three or four guys would get pissed up and try to come and buy a blow job from me. I tried to make it look like it didn't bother me, but it did. The people knew of it. I tried talking about it with my supporters. I'd relapse in the end. I found that particular incident to be the most humiliating. A continuous strain would loom over me throughout my addiction. Year after year I would sacrifice another beating or be hurt by someone who obviously hated themselves so much they would injure or seriously hurt someone else so they could feel better about themselves.

Drugs and drug users, and the behaviour from using aren't all evil.

Using drugs masks who I really am.

I look into the mirror, and I see the outer me.

Inside, I hold the troubled, afraid, and defensive selves that hold some shame [for] what life dished out unfairly.

Leslie: Why do you want to make your story public?

Dee: I've never known not living the everyday, not knowing the awful things that have happened to me in my life. It's like I'm so stuck in being afraid and being hurt, and I've never been able to do anything about it. I guess, in a way, my story expresses what happened to me, how it happened, and who was responsible for it. A lot of it is fears that I'm ready to let go of, I guess. I never tried to hurt anybody else, but as a result of the addiction in my life, I have.

To be afraid and to be ashamed is internalized. It isn't a good feeling to have. It's really hard to get out of the unclean feeling of having to be a prostitute. I still have my regulars, but when I go out there and look at the street, it's nothing to hold your head up high about.

It's a dirty rotten occupation. I've never liked it.

It isn't what it once was—neither is the addiction, or the people, or the environment.

Why do you think these stories are important to tell?

This has been really therapeutic for me; I feel like I've grown up over the time that I've spent working on this.

Nobody's being hurt by this. I don't have a problem with everybody knowing these things. I'm hoping it will help other women get off the street because those were my most fearful and my most painful days.

I had one of my abusers confront me, and this was childhood abuse. He confronted me as an adult and I was really proud of him because he apologized for molesting me when I was ten. That being one of my biggest scars, I really took it to heart that he was sincere about his apology.

So, in a sense it is possible, you know?

For the rest I pray! (*Laughing*) I don't have a choice.

When fears are acknowledged, they are given back to the abuser.

I am no longer afraid.

Fears, yeah ...

Seven

TAMARA

EDITORS' INTRODUCTION

In "Changes," Tamara describes a childhood spent in the relatively privileged environment of a daughter in a "normal," middle-class white family living in a nice house on the affluent west side of Vancouver. As a young woman, Tamara aspires to be independent, successful, and attractive. Her drug use begins as youthful rebellion: exciting adventures with friends and lovers. As her milieu shifts from the legitimate business world to the illegal drug economy, she continues to pursue money, power, and love, desiring all the things media and advertisers tell us we need to be happy: money, cars, fancy clothes, and nice houses. Before she finds herself in the Downtown Eastside, Tamara shares many of the stereotypical mainstream assumptions about the neighbourhood and the people who live there. She imagines it as a place she would never inhabit.

Tamara's and other women's stories in *In Plain Sight* raise troubling questions about "drugs" and "legality" that belie simple answers. Why are some substances (heroin and cocaine) illegal, while others (alcohol and tobacco) are legal? The production, distribution, and consumption of illicit drugs is a multi-billion-dollar global industry, and the manufacturing and sale of licit drugs by transnational pharmaceutical corporations accounts for even more profits, trade, and employment. People in all walks of life take drugs to feel and not to feel, to eat and not to eat, to sleep and not to sleep, to arouse desire and to suppress it, to stimulate children and to calm them down. Fortunes are accumulated, relationships are transformed, and lives are shaped by drugs of all kinds, every day and everywhere. When mediating the experience of everyday life through legal and illegal drug use is the rule, not the exception—as it is in Canada and other western countries—what differentiates patients and recreational users from *addicts*? Doctors and pharmacists from *dealers*?

Few women occupy the upper echelons of the illicit drug economy. Most find themselves increasingly dependent on drugs and on the men who provide them (or the money needed to acquire them). Tamara's story tells of exploitation, subordination, and betrayal. She speaks of sudden changes that catch her off guard and send her reeling, of her life spiralling out of control yet punctuated, always and still, by moments of reflection and dreams of change. In her determination to hold herself accountable for what she describes as her own choices, Tamara holds on to her desire for autonomy and independence.

Changes

Edited from interviews conducted July 2001–December 2001
Interviewers: Denielle Elliot and Cathy Chabot

I had everything from the time I was, like, a baby.

Let's see, I was born in a small town in Alberta and then we moved to Point Grey.[21] I'd gone to a Catholic school in Alberta and I think I was four going on five in Grade 1 because of the way they structured the starting date. They started me early, anyway. We moved in with my mom's parents. They flew us out here and my dad was working. Then my parents bought a house two months later in Point Grey, where we grew up. The elementary school was, a block and a half away. Grades 1 to 7.

I remember when I was about three I had long hair, ringlets and bangs, and I always used to stick this bow, this Christmas bow, on my head. Fancy things. My sister had a little bit of hair, just enough hair on the top of her head to make a nice curl. I used to get so mad because I couldn't have a curl on my head. I got up one morning and cut it off. It was terrible. I felt guilty, so I started cutting my hair and I cut my bangs right off.

Then our little brother came along. A week before I turned ten, he was born. We looked after my brother a lot on the weekends, and we used to have fistfights. My sister would say, "It's your turn to get up," because we had the only little brother in the city that woke up at six in the morning. I remember that. "I got up with him yesterday! It's your turn now!"

My sister and I were really close, and we grew up fairly well off. We had everything! Ping-pong tables, pool tables. We had allowance and got paid for just about everything we did. It was horrible for later on because I still think that's why I have a hard time hanging on to money (*laughing*).

I remember one time we had fifty dollars. We couldn't go on this camping trip—my dad, something happened with my dad's car. I think he just didn't want to go camping. That was just the excuse; the car didn't just break down. We got fifty dollars each on top of our weekly allowance. We

---

21. Upper-class suburb of Vancouver.

took friends every single day to Playland and the PNE,[22] like the entire summer, and we still had money left over. We had our ritual popcorn, chips, and chocolate bars every night with our allowance money, and then we'd go to the same theatre down the street.

I remember that.

Every Christmas day at twelve or one, there'd be a herd of kids at the door because they wanted to see our presents and play with them. Our Christmas tree was always filled with presents. I thought all the kids got presents like that.

We just didn't know any different. Yeah, we had everything.

Me and my sister were so close in age we were almost like twins. We had to have the same thing, just different colours. My brother got spoiled rotten too 'cause he was the baby. We'd go to Frank Baker's. When I was a kid that was a treat and a half. For anybody that was a treat back then, but, you know, we got to go there on a weekly basis, and then on Fridays we'd go to Chinatown and Saturdays it would be somewhere else. We went out for dinner half the nights of the week, nice places, not just quick burgers and stuff.

So we grew up fine.

We had everything ... except—there was drinking in the family.

My mom would go out and buy these crystal vases. In this house they had these chandeliers; one was a swag, a three-tiered swag.

I remember that.

They got that and sold it for just under ten grand, but the one in the dining room was five-tiers, and every one was hand-cleaned. Oh, it was beautiful; it was just like you see in the movies! I remember, when I was little, even when I was three years old, they used to plunk a Sears catalogue in front of me, and by the time I was seven or eight I'd have my entire household on a list of what I was going to have by the time I was eighteen. I had it down to spoons and knives.

I thought it was this magical number—eighteen. That's the day you moved out and you had everything.

When I got into high school I started going out with friends who were older than me. When I was fourteen I was really quiet, really shy—nothing. All of a sudden, I just changed, literally overnight. My mom had a term for it. I was, like, "How dare you call me that!" I just changed.

---

22 The Pacific National Exhibition is an annual agricultural fair held in Vancouver. Playland is a seasonal mid-way with rides and entertainment held on the PNE grounds.

I met people that were older than me, like five or six years older, and I wanted to work and have money. It was always the money that was the factor there.

I wanted to live on my own—well, I did and I didn't.

I didn't realize how good I had it at home. I don't think anybody does until they move out.

But you know, in the case of downtown here, it's the other way around. I think some people leave home because it's better.

I started hanging around with these people that were older and then I just decided that I wasn't going to school. And I was getting A's and B's! I was really smart. But I decided I wasn't going to go. Technically, I was expelled because I didn't show up for three classes. I would have been fourteen in Grade 9, thirteen or fourteen. I was the first girl ever to quit school in Point Grey. I was the last one anybody would suspect. People couldn't believe it, "What happened to her?"

I smoked pot since I was fourteen. Acid was the first thing I did even before I smoked pot. I remember going down to Gastown and we were trying to panhandle. I remember people saying, "You're too well dressed. You have better clothes than I do! You shouldn't be panhandling!"

So that didn't work.

That was the mid-seventies. We were out tripping around on the weekends and we'd go back to a normal life on the weekdays. I don't know what changed that. Actually, I met this guy. It was a rebellious stage in my life.

My dad was mad, probably because I had a boyfriend … Oh, and the fact that he broke into our house three times …

We're running and screaming because we hear the balcony window open up, we grab the dog—a big Doberman—and we're running into my parents' room. My dad's going, "What are you bringing him in here for? Let him go!" So we let the dog go and the guy goes flying off the balcony. Then I go to introduce him to my dad. He's got a black leather jacket, a jean vest with a black leather swastika on the back. I thought my dad was going to kill me! So that was kind of the end of that. Then I met this Chinese guy.

I went out and got a job at a little hot spot restaurant down the street for two dollars and fifty cents an hour, which was forty cents more than the minimum wage. Oh, God, two ten an hour!

Oh, boy, I slaved away there!

We had a dishwasher since I was six years old and we used to complain about putting dishes in the dishwasher. It's all we had to do. Well, they didn't have a dishwasher at this restaurant. I had my elbows in a big stainless steel sink full of dishes and it was horrible! So I didn't work there that long. Then my dad decides that I have to pay room and board—a hundred a month.

I'm like, "I'm your daughter, how could you charge me?"

I decided that I should move out because I got a better job at a different restaurant down the street. My parents were always separating or getting back together. When they'd get back together they'd have all these rules. I worked until three in the morning and my parents wouldn't give me a key, but I knew how to get into locks with a bobby pin. We had twenty or thirty-some odd windows in the house. I told them that they must have left one of them unlocked and that's the one I got in last night. Then they started really doing a check and noticing that there were no windows left unlocked. My dad even started putting sticks in them to make sure I couldn't get in. But I was getting in.

He said, "Well, if you're not in by midnight, that's it. You have to move."

I said, "Well I can't, I work until three."

"Well, you're going to have to quit that job then, because we want you in by midnight."

I was going to keep this job; they weren't really going to kick me out. I guess my denial stage had started (*laughing*).

You don't want it to happen, so it's not going to.

One night we stayed out. I worked, and then at eight in the morning I went with my boyfriend's brother to Spanish Banks. We went sun tanning. Well, I fell asleep in the sun because I'd only had a few hours' sleep. I came back burnt like a lobster. Just burnt.

My dad says, "Well, just pack your bag. That's it, I told you to go."

"Dad, you can't do this like this!"

"Oh yes I can!" And so I started packing the suitcase.

"Oh, no, no, no—those suitcases belong here. No, no—you have to go buy your suitcases with your allowance if you want to do that, or with the money you've made."

I was just totally disgusted, so I grabbed two garbage bags full of stuff and took them up to my boyfriend's.

They were always asking me to move in, his parents.

Like I said, my boyfriend at the time was Chinese. I stayed at his place. I had a lot of Chinese people in my life from that point on. We all worked, we all had different jobs at this one place. We'd go to work and we'd go somewhere to eat after.

I found out that Chinese families were different from Canadian families. What we eat for a family of two fed their entire family of twelve people. I stayed there for nine months, and it was different. I could speak Cantonese, not fluently, but the mother didn't speak one word of English, not one word. She wasn't about to learn, either (*laughing*). It was just the way it was, so you had to learn Chinese phrases. I could speak pretty well.

When I was there, the oldest brother got injured. I remember that there were acupuncturists, all kinds of these Chinese doctors there day and night, for like a week. I remember that.

So anyway, that's when I moved out. I didn't speak to my parents for six months after that. I was, like, "How dare you!" I called them later, crying, wanting to move back home because I was starting to lose a bit of weight. I was always about a hundred and fifteen pounds, and I remember I went down to about a hundred and seven or eight. It was quite a weight drop in a couple of weeks. But my dad said, "No, no. You thought you knew everything. You knew it all and you want to come back in six months?"

So I never did call them. For six months I didn't, and then I started calling them again.

I got my own place [in the suburbs]. I remember it was like $185 a month. My parents bought me all the condiments; they spent 175 dollars on all this stuff, which was a lot of money back then. I had everything for the next year. Then I meet this guy that was friends with my boyfriend. I remember he used to come over with the best pot. I started going out with him and that just killed my boyfriend because we were kind of mutual friends. I ended up going out with him for seven and a half years. When he finished university, he moved in with me.

I was making twenty-five, thirty dollars a night in tips, which was good for a graveyard shift, and then I got a job cleaning for a company. I worked there for a year and a half, something like that. I made almost five dollars an hour; almost double the minimum wage. I worked there and I went back to upgrading at a vocational school. I think I got paid through the government to do it that way. I was never on welfare.

I didn't go on welfare until I was almost thirty.

I got my Grade 12 a month after I turned seventeen. Then I took some more classes and worked as a clerk typist. I applied at a large corporation and I was hired, and really did well there. I was actually making pretty good money when I started. I think I was only seventeen, and I was still clearing around $1600 a month. I had to work evening shifts; four to eleven or eight to two used to be good because they'd send you home in a taxi.

About half way through that year, they switched to a computerized system so my hours got cut back drastically; I was only working, like, two days a week. I remember having a hard time paying my rent, even though my rent was only two fifty a month. I remember just kind of struggling there for a while. I'd come home and eat rice and a meat pie. I swore I'd never look at another meat pie again. But I learned a lot.

I took a lot of courses and I had a lot of options available. I could have gone into journalism. I used to do things for the newspaper and I worked in security, not as a security guard but in fraud. I worked in fraud for many years and I ended up taking the customer service route.

I wanted to get into outside sales.

I was living the high life. It was fun.

I remember never having a drop of extra time; I could do it all. Now I'm always late, but then I could get it all done (*laughing*).

I worked at this company and I belonged to Toastmasters—public speaking—and I'd go to Distinct Quality Circle, which initially came from Japan. It was like management and employees working together for better work situations. Oh, God, what else did I do? Junior Achievement. This was all at the same time, and I was usually taking two night classes a week. I also took some writing classes.

So at this time I'm going out with "John."

I started going out with him two days before I started my new job with this corporation. Our whole relationship was competition. We couldn't even have a game of Risk together. We'd be the last two players and we wouldn't be talking. We would be ready to kill. He'd get 85 per cent in a marketing class, I'd have to have 87. I had to beat him.

We were just starting to get into the coke a bit. My ex-boyfriend used to come over. He said he had allergies. He was going to the bathroom all the time but what he was doing was snorting. Then finally I guess he couldn't keep it a secret anymore. That's how we started getting into it. To me coke and heroin were taboo. You didn't go near people who did it.

I remember once I was studying for this marketing exam. The class was so tough I couldn't handle it with a full-time job too. One assignment took ten hours. If you didn't get 75 per cent in the mid-term you had to drop out. Me and two other girls got higher than that. I remember studying for that exam, and John comes out and says, "Do you want some coke? It's up to you, I don't want to sway you either way."

I'm going, "Should I or shouldn't I?"

God! I didn't know all this stuff yet!

I said I'd do a couple of lines. I got 98 per cent on that exam. I thought it was the coke that got me that mark. It wasn't, but that's what I believed. I really believed that. It was horrible.

I probably snorted it five times and then I started freebasing.

I didn't think I had a problem.

I'd been smoking pot since I was fourteen. I'd done acid, MDA, meth, mescaline—you know, stuff like that, dabbled in those kind of things. I probably didn't even smoke pot for a couple of years. "Oh, pot makes you stupid, forget it, you know, too slow."

I was always an over-achiever. The whole time I was with this company I was an over-achiever.

So I started getting into coke, but it wasn't on the street level at all, thank God! I took twenty years to get there (*laughing*). It was a social thing, but I think now I'm trying to understand that it probably was a little more than a social thing.

You see I was the one that held my family together. I was the one ... everything. You know, I was always an over-achiever. I had to be better than everyone, always, always. I couldn't fail at anything; that was just unheard of. When I started getting into coke I was bored with my life. The coke life was a fast, fast life. I was meeting a whole different crowd of people.

That's when I was living the good life, I guess.

Here's me going to work at the corporation and I was freebasing for about a year. Nobody knew I was doing it. I was just snorting in public and basing in private. I was living in this false little world. I was screwing up and didn't know it.

I started basing 800 dollars a day, me and my ex-boyfriend. Then I started selling it. I was getting really good money and I was selling pot and hash too.

So I was living the high life when I was twenty-one.

My mom and dad divorced and sold the house. My dad ended up with this other lady. He lived in another part of Vancouver for a few years, and my sister and I got a luxury townhouse. It was one of the nicest ones there. It was like $600 a month, and the next year it went up to $750 a month. It was beautiful.

I took my brother in when I was going on twenty-one. My brother would have been ten going on eleven. I took him away from my mom; I went to welfare and got custody of him, temporary custody. They kept telling Mom, "You don't have to do this, you know." But my mom decided to do it because she was drinking. I was like, "Oh, my God! Don't have another drink Mom. Just don't have another drink. It's that simple."

I was not helpful to my mom at all that way because I didn't understand. I didn't. Years later I needed my mom's help and I didn't get it. To this day I still have a problem calling her. I haven't called in a year, not at all. She's older now and it's really sad. I've got to get off this. My mom has not drank to this day; it's been, like, twenty some odd years.

So, I became bored with my job, and I was bored with my relationship. Every year in the mail I received a notice: "In the year 2003 you will be eligible for a pension." 2003 would have been early retirement at forty-three, and it was a nice-sized pension because I had contributions I was making on my own. That kind of screws me up because I could have been getting a nice little pension now, it really would have been more than I'm getting on welfare.

We won't talk about that because I'm not getting it (laughing).

But I remember that job being like a jail sentence. You know, we weren't even in the nineties yet, just late seventies, early eighties, and the year 2003 ...

I'm, like, "Oh my God! Is this it? This is my life with this corporation? This is it?"

I always wanted something more.

I decided there's better in life. I was just so bored.

There's got to be better.

I stayed at the company a bit longer and then I guess I got mixed up with people in the drug trade—but, like, way up there! I had never even been on the street down here, never. I wouldn't even get off the bus anywhere near skid row. I just started getting mixed up. I started selling drugs myself, like larger amounts, pot, coke—not heroin. I stayed away from heroin.

It was unreal. I had money to go do anything I wanted.

I was selling but it wasn't like a full-time job. By the end of the morning I had all my money. I always had people that would sell it for me, and I wasn't even counting the money. I always had a thousand bucks cash on me. I remember being stopped by these cops for a seat belt. It was some stupid ticket just to harass me. They knew I had money, and they knew I was probably dealing. I couldn't see that then, I thought it was just harassment. But I remember this cop wanting to count my money. The cops that brought me in made this other cop count everything, every last penny at the bottom of my purse. I had 999 dollars and ninety-four cents.

They attached a little note. "We couldn't see you leaving with such an odd amount. We put a collection together, put six cents in."

(Laughing) I walked out with a thousand.

I was getting into the wrong crowd, a sleazier kind of crowd, and they were just ripping me off. I don't mean ten or twenty dollars, I mean hundreds and thousands, and that would set me back a bit. I'd do it again and then somebody else would do it, and then it was like a whole little network of them. That's how they work, kind of like these ones downtown, but these ones downtown are not quite as quick.

These were pretty fast people, that's what was destroying me.

I felt I had nowhere to go. I was trying to do it on my own and I couldn't. I couldn't, I couldn't.

I know that now but I didn't then.

I was trying to keep afloat without anybody knowing I was suffering.

One day I had to go out of town because I didn't know people who sold grams or packages. I had to sell eight-balls and up. Then it was hard getting eight-balls, it was quarters[23] and up. Then it was halves and up.

I didn't realize it was dangerous. I met this guy. I watched him fix and I was turning grey watching him flag the blood. He was looking at me going, "I'm the one who's supposed to be going down here, not you."

I couldn't even go for a blood test without passing out.

He said, "I can get you eight-balls." I remember paying twice the price; I didn't care. I fell head over heels in love. I gave him my brand new car. All these other criminals were saying, "He's not the nice guy you think he is."

These guys saw me coming. I'd never been around junkies other than the guy that I'd watched fix. I had no idea. I always had dope and I always gave it away; I never used it to bribe people.

So we went through an eight-ball and then I felt sick.

I remember them saying, "Well, we'll fix you."

I'm going, "Well, don't you have a new needle?"

No.

One of the guys said, "She's one of these rich bitches who wants her own."

Of course I wanted to fit in, and this guy looked totally healthy, but the biggest scare back then was hepatitis. This was the eighties.

I got hepatitis B the first time I fixed, and I was healthy, really healthy. I knew that's where I got it because I had only fixed one time. I saw the same family doctor I'd had since I was five. She didn't have a clue, she was close to retiring. It was kind of embarrassing, actually. I remember my car was yellow. I had a yellow dress on, and my eyes went yellow.

I got over the hepatitis B; in six weeks I was healthy.

---

23. Quarter ounce.

Once I started fixing I loved it. That beat any freebase toke; I can't even explain the high.

At that point in my life I was always two months ahead signing up for my classes. I was so organized. I think it was an escape for me because I was always the family mediator; I was the mediator for everything. I couldn't screw up. When I started fixing, my friends were saying, "You're going to start getting skinny."

As soon as I started fixing I started getting skinnier.

At that time you didn't fix. Nobody had respect for junkies at all. It was made really clear; you could base it, you could snort your nose off, but you couldn't fix it.

What's the difference? It all goes in the same way.

I remember just loving it, thinking that was it.

I was working as a high-powered executive and I was arrogant then. I got stopped by this cop, and he charged me with impaired. I was not impaired but I couldn't beat it because I didn't know. There was no breathalyzer taken, and I still lost my license. So I went to this drug treatment program and there were only two people there who were on welfare, the rest were all professional people. I was still with the corporation. I get there and three other employees were there (*laughing*).

I was straight after that because I was trying to hold a good image for my boyfriend.

I was doing really well at my job and everything, and I was staying away from the dope. I'd do it at Easter, Christmas, my birthday. But compared to when I first got into it ...

My little brother died. That's when everything happened.

It was quite a bad time for me in my life.

Everything was a big change, right then. Pretty bad.

He would have been fifteen going on sixteen, and I was twenty-five, twenty-six, something like that. He was hit by a car. I remember, just a couple of months before he died, he'd come and clean my whole apartment. He did my clothes and folded them in my laundry basket.

I was like, "Wow! My brother did all this!"

I never had time to thank him. It was always too late when I was coming in.

When my brother died, I took a leave from the corporation about three weeks later. I had been there for eight and a half years. I broke up with John after eight years of being together, then I realized maybe it isn't so good being by myself after all. I was so used to always being with somebody. It was the feeling of abandonment—even though I broke up with him, it was still a feeling of abandonment. I was still really prim and proper.

Those changes were because of my brother. Plus, I was making more money selling the dope.

I saw this psychic a week after my brother died, and everything that she said was going to happen for the next seven years came true. Everything. I remember she said, "There is something left untold, something left unsaid."

And there was.

The day he died he continuously called, as though he needed to tell me something. I kept putting him off; I was too busy.

After I saw the psychic, I was at a party and I was still extremely upset over the sudden loss. A friend took me home to watch movies and have company and get my mind off things. Later that evening I looked away from the TV and saw my brother sitting there, the way he used to, resting his chin on his hand. I could see through him but I could see the colour of his clothes. It was almost like he wanted me to remember him, as he was dressed at a wedding, the week before he died. The medium said there would be a sign that he had made it to his new existence.

After that, I decided not to use any drugs on the anniversary of his death and on his birthday.

I started getting hitched up with these losers. They were just horrible, horrible. I was shooting coke and I met this young guy. I knew him for about a year.

He said, "I've got these two guys that want to meet a girl, and they're coming out of jail and they want to set something up."

I'm going, "What do they want. If they just want a girl ... "

I didn't understand any of that then, I just didn't.

I was totally, 100 per cent clueless when it came to that.

So I met these two on a Saturday morning at a restaurant. One was this little old guy who talked with his mouth covered. When I met him I was totally mesmerized. It was like watching a movie without the film, without the visuals, the stories this guy had. He was brilliant. I learned a lot with these guys. I really did, especially the old guy. I actually really miss him.

When I got set up, they wanted a girl that was not just familiar with the street but knew some business. Apparently, they wanted someone to take over this apartment that they had. Instead of using a hotel to have their meetings, they wanted a place that was straight. I couldn't have anybody over who drank a lot or used. At first, they said they would pay up to 400 dollars for rent, but I looked at this place that was about $650, and I thought, "Well, if they're paying four, I'll throw in the other two-fifty." I was on leave from the company then, I took a sick leave and I was getting about $950 a month—which is way more than I'm getting now.

What happened was, I moved there three weeks later. Originally, I wasn't supposed to tell anybody about this move. I told three people. One person was straight, one was right into everything, and the third one was a user. All three of them said, "Don't go we'll never see you again. You're getting way too big."

But I went.

At that time I thought, "Well, my life's so topsy-turvy right now, how much worse could it get?"

That's how all that started.

When I met them, that's when I got into the heroin.

They put heroin in a crystal dish; it was K3. K5 is already processed, the highest quality. K4 is, like, the next one down. That's when they used to cap it.

I'd just started fixing myself, and I wasn't that good at it yet.

So these guys were saying, "With your permission, we're going to get you a little bit wired and then get you sick so you can see what a junkie goes through so you know our business."

I said, "Sure." I was thinking, "Oh, sure, I wouldn't mind. I'll try it."

I wasn't even thinking that heroin was addictive. I had done heroin once in my freebasing days. I didn't know anything about heroin. I thought it was kind of like coke.

I remember meeting this guy who went all the way up to Prince George to get off it. I couldn't understand him, "Why didn't you just quit?" That was my attitude. That was my attitude to my mom's drinking, too. I didn't understand.

Just before I met these two, after my brother died, my mom was always blaming me for killing my brother. I'd say, "He got killed in a car accident." That's when my relationship with my mom kind of stopped for a while.

I had never lived in East Van, and that's where I was set up in this apartment. So I moved there, which to me was horrifying.

I saw this bunch of kids—teenagers and a little bit older, hanging around the Seven-Eleven a block away, and I'm, like, "Oh, my God! I'm never going outside after seven o'clock." I was scared living down there. I really was! I just wasn't used to seeing mobs of people hanging out, and I was, like, "Oh, my God, there are little gangs down here. This is East Van, oh, my, God!" Right in the thick of things, you know? Oh, that was funny. I was scared to go out (laughing).

All of the sudden, one day, everything changed.

I came home from the store. I went to buy some vegetables because the guys were expecting an old friend, and they bought this sturgeon. They were going to cook this sturgeon some special way, and I was really looking forward to this. We had all the food laid out, and we had this cognac. I came home because I forgot something, and there were all these guys in jeans, some in suits.

I thought, "Wouldn't I have had some notice if all these guys were coming?" There was like ten or twelve of them in my place. I'm walking in and nobody is saying anything to me. I'm looking at the old guy, like, "Who are these people?"

He goes, "It's the police."

One of them said, "Just stand over there. We'll be out of here in a few minutes."

Then they said, "Is there anything else here?"

The old man went over to my kitchen drawer and pulled out a quarter ounce of heroin. I never knew it was there! That was the one time they left something in my place.

Well, that was the start of the next forty-five days.

I was always told, "If you want to live like a princess or a queen, you can." I did, believe me. I went out for these lunches every day, elaborate lunches. And clothes, I wasn't allowed to buy stuff from used places but it was like a bad habit. I had to go and see what kind of deals I could get. It was just like an addiction. I had to go and get all these deals.

I'd come back and say, "Oh, somebody gave it to me." They had this philosophy that somebody might have died in them so that's why you weren't allowed to buy used clothes.

Then all of the sudden everything changed.

My rent had been paid, everything was paid for me, then I got cut off. So there I was. I had never worked on the street, didn't really know how to do anything but sell drugs, and I'd moved away from the area where I used to do that. After that forty-five days, it was just wild how everything happened. I was devastated, actually, because I had never spent that much time with people. It was like I was being brainwashed—not brainwashed, but I was constantly being told things, over and over.

It was like watching a movie.

So both the guys got arrested. Then I spent the next four years with another guy. Originally, it was, "No one's to touch the girl." Well, I ended up being with this guy, it just happened.

Things changed.

The old guy was writing to me and telling me why I couldn't stay with my boyfriend, "This is what's going to happen if you stay with him."

To this day, everything he said was going to happen did happen. It was really creepy.

I moved. By that point, I was working with a different company in a totally new field. I was like a minnow with sharks. The people I was doing business with were worse than drug dealers ... my dad kept saying, "You're no different. You might as well get back into the drugs. The kind of people you're dealing with, you're going to end up dead."

In my relationship I was like the caretaker; this guy couldn't take care of himself, he was institutionalized. I'd never known stories of abuse, and this guy, as the stories came out—it was horrible! At that time I started seeing my mom every week. On Sunday I'd go there for dinner.

I couldn't understand not knowing your mother.

I got charged with a really serious crime against my boyfriend.

It felt degrading; there I was in the courtroom, in my working clothes. There was my mom and my sister sitting up in the courtroom. I talked to them the night before on the phone. My mom had said I could come and stay with her if I had to. So I'm telling my story to the judge, telling him that, and there's my sister shaking her head "no."

My self-esteem at that time was really low. I thought, "What kind of a nice guy would go out with a girl that has been charged with such a horrendous crime?"

Oh, my God! How could I explain that?

From the time I was charged to the preliminary hearing, I really felt that that was my last couple of months of freedom. I was actually convinced I was going to do several years.

I started going out with guys that were really abusive. I didn't really understand anything about abuse. The first time I'd ever heard that word was probably when I was twenty-six. I remember a lawyer saying, "It's abuse, it's abuse you're going through."

I was like, "How dare you say that to me! I have never been in an abusive relationship or abusive situation. How dare you! That's not it at all."

So I just totally ignored it, and from that point on I started going into abusive relationships, not realizing what they were. I couldn't see it.

Sometimes I still think I can't, but I'm getting better. I'm much better now.

There was five thousand dollars bail, and I was ordered to move home with my dad. I hadn't lived at home since I was fourteen! All of the sudden there I am, I'm ordered to go home and live with my dad and his wife. My dad was—I guess he was dealing with his own shock.

He was, like, "Go to sleep and get up and look for a job."

My mom was not supportive, not at all. She kept saying, "Well, you should have listened to me."

I was partying like it was my last few months of freedom. Partying, like really partying. Drinking, going out, I wouldn't get a stable place; I was just living here and there. It got worse, though.

There were guys that said, "Either put out or get out."

I'd say, "Okay, where's the door? I'm getting out."

It was escalating from there, I kept meeting guys that were deeper and deeper into crime, but every guy became more and more abusive, not so much physically as psychologically.

Finally, at my preliminary hearing, the judge said, "There's no judge or jury in this country that would convict a girl of such a crime against someone like that."

I guess this judge had tried him many, many years before that.

My esteem got lower and lower and lower, and I actually got back together with this same guy. It jeopardized my relationship with my father. My father said, "You go back with him—don't call me! Look at everything we've done for you."

I went years and years before I ever called my father again.

The next thing you know, my boyfriend's getting himself put back in jail, which, I guess, in retrospect, was a good thing to do.

I got a place over by Broadway; it was this cute little bachelor suite. Then I started meeting all these creepy, creepy people. They were losers—big-time losers—but of course I didn't know that.

It was all about action. It was all fun and danger.

I went away with this one guy, and my friend was there, saying, "Don't go. You shouldn't go." We took off to another province, and this guy got picked up by the police. That was the first time I'd really seen street life—hookers and everything, druggies—street level. I'd never seen street-level people.

Oh, my God, was that an eye-opener!

I met this girl, I remember letting her have a bath at my place. She was so appreciative. I didn't know until I ended up on the street years later how nice that was when someone let you have a shower or bath. Such simple things make a big difference in someone's life. She was really nice. She's dead now.

She had all of her clothes taken and I had everything of mine taken too, all my clothes, a picture of my brother, things I had from my grandmother when I was seven. My boyfriend took all of that because I told him I couldn't be with him. There was just too much trouble around him.

I almost died then, that was in '89. My liver and spleen were shutting down. That's when I was diagnosed; they called it non-A, non-B[24] then. I didn't get it from fixing; they don't know how I got it. I remember being really sick and phoning my dad.

He said, "Do you want a plane ticket or a bus ticket?"

I said, "A bus ticket."

It took me sixteen hours to get back, and I only drank half a cup of apple juice. I was so sick. Within days they said, "You're really sick, you've got two weeks to pull through or you won't make it."

For three months I couldn't stay up for more than four hours a day. It was horrible. I had no place to stay, they had no hospital beds, and there was really nothing they could physically do other than give me dextrose intravenously. They told me how to mix up the dextrose and inject it to keep sugar going through my blood because I wasn't going to be able to eat. I had to go every second day for blood tests, like I'm talking eight vials every second day!

I got better and I got this place on Hastings. I met these guys and they started giving me grams of heroin. I was selling it for 1100 dollars a gram back then and taking nothing out. It was pure. Then I started using one gram a day.

I got so wired. I was really screwed up for a while.

I remember crawling up the stairs one day, and these guys were setting me up to rob me. I was there by myself with that much dope. I was getting two grams a day; then I was getting four a day. I started screwing up. One guy started stealing my dope when I was nodding off. I owed money. I called my old friends and it ended up that these guys apologized for getting me into it!

Phew! I was scared. I was really scared. But not scared enough to sell my body.

A few months rolled by and I'm broke. I had spent all my money and drank like a fish in the bar. In that time, I knew this girl on my floor, and I didn't know she was a trannie for a long time. She looked better than any girl. She gave me clothes to wear; she gave me this red spandex top and a little red skirt and red shoes, black jacket. I looked really good then. I was about 125 pounds.

When I started, I was hooking by the Waldorf Hotel.

---

24. Hepatitis C.

So there I was, and the first night I made a lot of money in three hours. It was fast. I remember thinking I should have been doing this years ago.

There was a young kid I met, he was filthy rich; he was my brother's age. He picked me up and he said, "You know what? You're going to end up downtown one day."

I said, "No, never."

He said, "You will."

I wouldn't associate with downtown people then.

A lot of the girls down here started out hooking really young. That was the last thing on my mind. I was twenty-eight when I started hooking; I wasn't young. A lot of women just end up being put in positions—especially if they're wired. I don't think it really matters down here what it is.

It's like a guy said to me the other day, "There's always that little man inside of you that says, 'No, no, don't—that's danger. Don't do that. Don't do this.'"

After a while you just start forgetting about that, and that little guy doesn't come out anymore. Anything could happen.

I started working and I started buying heroin again. I used to have my steak and lobster dinner every night, nine o'clock sharp. I'd already had my coke and I'd have my heroin after dinner. I was probably doing twenty caps a day but I had the money. I had never been dope sick except for the time when those guys wanted me to know how it felt.

I lived pretty good then and I didn't realize it.

Then this guy from the old days shows up and decides he's going to get me to move up by the Sky Train into another area of town.

I thought I was in another city! I didn't even know where I was; I hated it.

I started getting robbed. I'd keep my money hidden but I was held up all the time. My boyfriend started taking my leather coats hostage. He didn't care what happened to me. He just told me to get back out there and work. So I got out of there and moved over to stay at this other guy's house.

I got myself off the heroin, and I got wired again helping this guy out. Stupid. I got charged with heroin then, that's the only charge I have.

After I left him another guy took me out of town, and I was trying to kick my heroin habit.

I stayed with him for three weeks and I got off the heroin. I did coke, just steady. He filled me full of cocaine until I couldn't do any more, until I was sick of it. Then I came back to Vancouver and got a room for seventy bucks a day, way back then. They charged me the full rate because they knew I could make the money. These pimps lived around there. I'd never had an experience with pimps before that other than the ones that pulled up and said, "Hey babe!"

I'd say, "I'm sorry, you can't afford me."

You didn't stand on the same corner as the girls who were with them. I remember talking to one girl. I came by around five in the morning and said, "Oh, my God, you're still here?"

She said, "Well, I haven't made my quota yet."

"Your quota?"

"Six hundred dollars."

I went back to heroin bit by bit, by bit. I was bored! I had all this money and nothing to do. Back then there were only certain dealers, you went to their houses. I would never come downtown! I guess at that time I was wired for nine months.

I met another guy from a different element and lived a different life. I was quite sheltered, and it was a really abusive relationship. On the surface, I was the envy of thousands, but inside, it was actually just abuse. This person would verbally abuse me for hours and hours and hours. He was an addict, a really bad addict. It got to the point where I wouldn't go anywhere; I wouldn't even go to the store. I was at the point where I almost gave up, then I thought I had to make a change, "I'm not letting this person do this." I went to detox and I came out on my birthday and moved in with some close friends of the guy I was with, thinking that they understood what was happening. They were really well off, extremely well off, hadn't really dealt with that side of life.

Well, it wasn't what I thought, and I didn't stay.

It was pretty crazy after that. I almost got killed by another guy I fell madly in love with. It was too wild and I told the guy, "We're from different sides of the tracks."

He just couldn't handle it. In a short relationship of three weeks I had broken ribs, black eyes.

I was thinking I had to leave town, and I met this young guy from overseas. At that time I could only tell him about a tenth of what I was doing because it would scare any normal person away. It was interesting; he kind of saved me in a lot of ways, and he learned a lot too. I recovered in three weeks; this little guy looked after me while I kicked the heroin. I didn't go to the hospital because I had a stupid little warrant for not showing up in court. I thought I'd go to jail if I went to the hospital.

I still felt like I needed to get away, so I went across Canada by bus, truck, whatever. I decided to do it not hooking. I decided to do it right. I had twenty dollars cash, that's all the cash I had. With one truck driver, the further south we got into the States, the more verbally abusive he got. He kept thinking I was going to sleep with him, and finally I said, "If I was sleeping my way across Canada, I'd be flying, not riding in your truck!" (*Laughing*)

I was gone almost a year; I went to Ontario and then I went all through the States. I did that straight. I was straight. I didn't do any dope. I drank like a fish though. It took me three truck rides to get back home from Thunder Bay, Ontario.

When I came back, I thought about contacting my old friends, then I thought, "No, no, that was a past thing in my life." I went to a shelter and, within a week, I had a place, a really tiny place.

I met all new friends but I had warrants, all these little warrants had added up. I wouldn't go visit anybody or get a ride home, I was afraid about getting stopped in a roadblock. I always took a taxi home, wore sunglasses and a hat.

Everybody would walk by, "Hi, Tamara." Oh, God! (*Laughing*)

One person said, "You know, you're not one of the ten most wanted. There's not APBs with eight by tens of you out on the corner!"

I applied for seven jobs. One was in a newspaper company; one was waitressing so I could get tips in cash. I could have had all the jobs. I hadn't worked a real job in ... how many years?

I took the waitressing job, of all the stupid things to do.

I made really good money. The owner was really into karaoke and we used to go partying all the time together. I turned myself in for my warrants, and I was put on probation. It seemed like I was on probation for five years! I was reporting weekly.

Then I met this guy—I guess it was the dangerous side again, the unknown, I think that's what always attracted me. People that I know from ten years ago still remember the day I met him. "You were doing great until you met him. You were doing just great!"

Anyway, I was straight then and I thought he was fooling around on me. I was getting mad and thinking he was fooling around, but the affair he was having was with heroin.

I left town to be with him and I ended up putting myself back on the street and getting wired again. My whole life was in shambles, everything I had put back together.

I left my job. I ended up leaving my group of friends and I was back on the street with this guy. I really, really liked this guy, and that was my whole life at that point. I was working by myself on the street. I wasn't working downtown. I guess that was a good thing because it was more money, plus I was healthy, I wasn't doing coke. I looked good. I made good money. I was spending anywhere from eight to fifteen hundred a day on heroin for the both of us. That was my life.

I got tired of it after six or seven years.

My life revolved around him, the customers, and the dealers.

That was my life.

I never had a Christmas, Easter, nothing. I remember resenting it. I missed my family; never saw anybody. I couldn't do anything because I was always paying for the heroin, every day. All I wanted was to get in touch with my family. You wake up Christmas Day dope sick so you can't go see your family, you have to wait until it's a bit later; by that time, they've probably had turkey dinner. I couldn't understand why this guy couldn't see that, but he had been wired for twelve years.

I guess I got fed up and started tripping around on my own. It didn't matter where I'd find a place, he'd move across the street, next door, upstairs, and still have me paying for the heroin. It was easy to pay for it. I paid for his friend for three years too.

I broke my ribs because I started passing out all the time. I was doing eight quarter-gram fixes a day. That's two grams a day. At certain times I would just drop to the ground.

One time I dropped, I ended up with broken ribs but it took two weeks to realize that because of the heroin I was doing. I wasn't dope sick an awful lot then; I always had money. I woke up one Saturday morning and it felt like somebody had stabbed me in the ribs. I remember lying there for four days and my ex lived upstairs.

He wouldn't help, not even twenty dollars.

The police came over because they heard through the grapevine that I was really hurt. I remember they said to him, "We saw her out there every day for how many years and we never saw you [heroin] sick once. If that's how you want to play, there's going to come a day when you're down." They thought it was just disgusting.

I forget who came by, but I finally ended up going to the hospital. A girlfriend came by, and by this time I was so heroin sick I couldn't even walk. She gave me heroin and I couldn't even feel it. I went to the hospital and I was there almost a month.

He didn't come to the hospital once, not once, to see me.

But I was glad.

That's where I met the methadone doctor. First, the doctors got me mixed up. My name was the same as four other patients and they thought I was living downtown here. "I want you to come to the pharmacy seven days a week." First thing, I get off the bus [in the Downtown Eastside] and I run into all these dealers saying, "Up? Down?"—How cruel! The first step I take, my feet aren't even on the ground, and there's dope in front of me.

Methadone stabilized my life.

I decided to get a place again in the area where I had been working on the street. I still had regulars. I tried keeping my distance from my ex but I still couldn't get rid of him. I had always supported him financially. It was getting nasty, so I moved downtown.

I never thought I'd ever live downtown, I never thought I'd come downtown. But, "Where's the one place he won't come?" Downtown.

So I went to a shelter and got a place. It was a fairly decent place, all renovated. I think I was the only junkie in the whole building. I stayed there three years.

When I came downtown, I started hanging around with different people. I had never hung around with other girls; it was always guys, but I got tired of paying for men (laughing). I still kept to myself, met a few people. I didn't hang out at the bars, I started volunteering, doing this and that, working part-time.

There's people from everywhere down here, everywhere.

I used to stereotype but I've realized there's all kinds of people living down here. I've met people who have been all over the world. Some of them have huge pensions and of all the places they could live, they live here. *They* aren't poverty-stricken, there's more money down here than in most places. Everything down here is geared to the drug trade. Everything.

I'm at the point now where I have to really pick and choose. I've realized that my addiction was not an addiction. Everybody who's employed in the drug trade, whether it's the dealers, the counsellors, the doctors—they say, "Well, you have this, it's addiction, or it's this or that." No, it isn't. It's all about having a choice. I think after all these years; the dope wasn't really the thing. The addiction covered and hid everything else.

I don't mind being down here. I think I've probably learned more about people and how they react and why they react. I don't know where I would move to if I had to move. I think it would depend on how much money I had. Everybody thinks if you move away from here, you'll be away from the drugs. Well, it's not true. If you move out of this area you get better quality drugs, everything's better.

It's not about drugs; you don't get stuck down here because of drugs. I moved here because of the changes in my life.

Leslie: Why do you want to make your story public?

Tamara: This is the first time I've looked at my life since I got into the drugs. This is the first time I've looked into anything. I wouldn't say I've been 100 per cent honest with myself here (*laughing*). But I'd have to say I've been at least half, a little bit more than half, at least it's something. If I could have done this ten years ago, who knows where I would have been?

I was normal; middle-class, both parents worked so we were more fortunate than most. We had money so it was a normal life, a good life— the envy of most people. I was the envy of a lot of people, but then a couple of times my life just changed. I'm not just saying a little bit of a change, like, a total change. Everything just went upside down. At one point, one day of my life would be like a month or two months of other people's. I was living so fast it was horrible. It was fun at the time. I guess I had never really experienced anything fearful before, as a child.

I think this story will maybe help someone make a decision as to what they want to do.

It's not necessarily wrong the way I did it. If I were to do it again I would go about it much differently.

I would do it differently—without a guy.

What do you want people to hear in your story?

You know if you want money, it's always there. There's money everywhere and you can do anything you want, you can work as a sex trade worker, you can do dope, but everything has its time and place.

You can do all of it and live a straight life, you can still have your holidays and go places and still meet that kind of people if you want, but you have to have a balance. You have to have a balance. I didn't. I went from one extreme to the other and got stuck.

Everyone does have a choice. Right now, at this time in my life, it's just a cycle, it's not like I don't care, but it's always tomorrow.

You know what? Tomorrow never does come if you keep saying that. I still procrastinate, I still do all the same things I did before; I guess those are the things that have to be changed. I think if you change those things then the drugs will change, everything else will change.

It's so situational. Everything changes, right?

EDITORS' AFTERWORD

In Plain Sight has presented difficult narratives—they were difficult to tell, they are difficult to read, and we, as editors, had difficulty working through the issues of representation that surround them. The women who published their stories here are not scholars, or professional writers. They are individuals who are materially disadvantaged, socially and culturally stigmatized, and politically excluded. Some have had access to formal education and others have not.

Readers will have found neither idealized nor demonized images of "the junkie," "the prostitute," "the underclass hero," "the victimized woman," "the AIDS sufferer," or "the homeless Aboriginal woman" in these accounts. Rather than these conventionalized figures, you will have met seven women exhausted by their daily struggles who have for reasons of their own, chosen to tell you their stories.

To some extent these narratives depict the journeys that accompany a particular lifestyle, but it is important to note the milestones by which the narrators themselves have marked their progress. They have shared accounts about hitting "rock bottom." They have judged themselves harshly for their actions, and their testimonies are intended to ward off any delusions about the exoticism of street life—romanticized representations sometimes found in the work of artists and poets who "drop into the life" for moments of inspiration, or in the work of advocates and researchers who try to challenge stigmatizing stereotypes.

The seven narrators *In Plain Sight* are individuals who want to contribute to public discussions about poverty, "the drug problem," sexism, racism, colonialism, health, illness, and violence. Their exclusion from public discourse precludes the circulation of their sometimes-alternative viewpoints generated through personal experiences. Several of the narrators have in the past spoken publicly on topics and social issues that most affect them. They are acutely aware of an editor's hand in the sculpting of text, sound, and/or image bites, and they recognize the absence of their own words in popular media.

We understand that ineffective presentation by we editors or failed witnessing on the part of some readers may result in further recriminations. In ultimately deciding to publish, we—editors and narrators—returned to the women's motivations, to their desire to be heard and seen, to tell their own truths in their own words. Now that this book has been published, will telling their stories put women at greater risk of local reprisals, of further stigmatization, of increased social exclusion? Will speaking frankly about hard times and hard choices reinforce rather than challenge negative stereotypes? Will the narrators' courage in acknowledging their mistakes be used as evidence to hold them responsible for poverty, the legacies of colonialism, and the denigration of women, all of which shape their lives but are not of their own making? Is publishing this book yet another act of voyeurism, no different, really, from the media sensationalizing we criticize? How do we responsibly present and understand narratives about lives not typically valourized by history, biography, or community memoir? These questions will remain open and troubling.

Leslie A. Robertson and Dara Culhane
Vancouver, February 2005

SELECT REFERENCES FOR ADDITIONAL READING

Baxter, Sheila. *No Way to Live: Poor Women Speak Out.* Vancouver: New Star Books, 1988. Photographs by Lori Gabrielson.

————. *Under the Viaduct: Homeless in Beautiful British Columbia.* Vancouver: New Star Books, 1991.

Benoit, Celia, D. Carroll and M. Chaudhry. "In Search of a Healing Place: Aboriginal Women in Vancouver's Downtown Eastside." *Social Science and Medicine*, vol. 56(4) (2003): 821–833.

Blomley, Nicholas. *Unsettling the City: Urban Land and the Politics of Property.* New York: Routledge, 2004.

Campbell, Burt. *The Door Is Open: Memoir of a Soup Kitchen Volunteer.* Vancouver: Anvil Press, 2001.

deVries, Margaret. *Missing Sarah: A Vancouver Woman Remembers Her Sister.* Toronto: Penguin Canada, 2003.

Kimley, Laurel and Jo-Ann Canning-Dew. *Hastings & Main: Stories from an Inner City Neighbourhood.* Vancouver: New Star Books, 1987. Portraits by Kenneth K. Stewart.

Sommers, Jeff and Nick Blomley. "The Worst Block in Vancouver." In *Every Building on 100 West Hastings*, edited by Stan Douglas, 18–61. Vancouver: Arsenal Pulp Press, 2002.

Taylor, Paul (ed). *The Heart of the Community: The Best of the Carnegie Newsletter.* Vancouver: New Star Books, 2003.

Woolford, A. "Tainted Space: Representations of Injection Drug Use and HIV/AIDS in Vancouver's Downtown Eastside." *B.C. Studies* (Spring 2001): 27–50.

APPENDIX 1: THE HEALTH & HOME RESEARCH PROJECT

The purpose of this appendix is to provide interested readers with an overview of the research processes from which *In Plain Sight* initially emerged. *In Plain Sight* grew out of a research project that began in 1999, funded by the Social Sciences and Humanities Research Council of Canada (SSHRC). The design and objectives of "The Health & Home Research Project" (Health & Home) reflected the federal government of Canada's official adoption of a "Population Health/Social Determinants of Health" pillar in their framework for health policy development.

The specific goals of the Health & Home Research Project were to conduct an inter-disciplinary longitudinal study of the relationships between health and housing among low-income women in Downtown Eastside Vancouver, and to do so through developing collaborative methodologies in which community women participated as researchers as well as research subjects. There is a considerable body of research that demonstrates that safe, secure, and sanitary housing is a necessary foundation for living a healthy life. Little research has been done, however, that focuses on how marginalized population groups like low-income, inner city women in Canada encounter structural barriers and systemic obstacles to finding and keeping adequate shelter, or to attaining and enjoying good health. Even less attention has been paid to what may be learned if members of such excluded groups tell their own stories in their own words, are listened to, and taken seriously.

Health & Home drew on the work of other researchers working in many places around the globe who are challenging conventional assumptions about social research. Laboratory-based, or experimental models developed by physical scientists are often considered a "gold standard" to which social scientists should aspire in conducting research. Central to this approach is the idea that researchers should be neutral observers who carry out purely objective research, and that research subjects (human and not) can be studied as if they are passive sources of value-free "data." Many social scientists argue that research conducted by human beings about other human beings differs in important ways from the physical sciences model drawn from research on inanimate or non-human objects of study. Acknowledging that social science is inevitably embedded in human relationships does not necessarily result in an abandonment of any rules or controls on research methodologies. Alternatives to "pure objectivity" need not simply be its mirror opposite: "pure subjectivity." Rather, social scientists increasingly employ a range of approaches from statistical surveys of large population samples and other quantitative methods, through interviews, life stories, researchers' observations and reflections, and other qualitative methods. Given that health and illness are simultaneously both individual *and* social experiences, interdisciplinary research teams who combine knowledge obtained through diverse research methods in an effort to understand human beliefs and practices in all their complexity are increasingly recognized as offering the greatest potential for creating the type of knowledge that can be effectively translated into action to alleviate health disparities.

The Health & Home Project subscribed to these new directions in health research and policy development, and the project as a whole was intentionally participatory and collaborative. We researchers did not see ourselves as neutral or objective observers documenting and analyzing the behaviour of passive objects. Rather, we recognized that we were engaged in a co-production of knowledge through dialogue with active, thinking, and experiencing subjects. Rather than claiming the singular expertise of discovery traditionally accorded scientists and academics, we wanted to utilize and transfer the skills we have gained through training and education, and share the authority we derive from our privileged positions. We hoped that our research would be useful in a variety of ways: from providing a few local women with training for potential employment in other research projects, to offering concrete suggestions for policy and program development to service providers, to broader and less easily measured goals of public education. But above all, we hoped to create a space for women to tell their stories, and to offer their analyses and recommendations.

The work of the Health & Home Project was distributed among four teams. These teams varied in size, but each was composed of faculty members, graduate students, and community-based researchers. The first research team conducted two structured interviews, one year apart, with eighty-five women in order to assess links between changes in housing situations and health status. The second worked with the boards of the two community partner organizations and interviewed board members and service providers. The third, a video team, trained five local women in basic videography and completed a twenty-two-minute video entitled *Building Bridges: A Housing Project for Women* that was screened at the 2003 Vancouver International Film Festival. The fourth, the ethnographic team, was subdivided into four smaller working groups that focused on interviewing women who were active drug users, consumers of mental health services, sex trade workers, and Aboriginal women, respectively.

Ethnography—literally, recordings (*graphy*) about people (*ethno*)—differs in its research methodology from sociological or epidemiological surveys, or journalistic investigation in some important ways. Survey researchers seeking statistical findings and generalizations across populations usually begin with previous academic research and/or priorities determined by governments and policy-makers. They develop questionnaires and provide multiple—but predetermined—answers that research subjects are asked to choose between. Or, alternatively, they may compose a set of inquiries requiring short answers, and conduct interviews based on questionnaires. Investigative journalists usually begin with issues that have become politically important, framed in ways that reflect the context and processes through which they have emerged in public discourse. Journalists utilize a range of methods similar to those that ethnographers employ, such as observation, open-ended interviews, photography, and film. While their work may conform to or challenge public perceptions, journalistic accounts most often use language, images, narrative structures, and styles that are familiar and easily accessible to their audiences. This is particularly the case when their subjects are groups of people or issues that have been deemed public problems.

Ethnographers, on the other hand, seek first to understand what research subjects themselves believe are significant research questions, and answers. We pay close attention to the ideas and biases that we as researchers bring to our work, and to what research subjects say about themselves, the contexts in which they live, and what they do in the practice of everyday life. We try to facilitate research subjects talking about their experiences and understandings in their own words and on their own terms.

The questions guiding Health & Home's ethnographic research were: "What do low-income women in Downtown Eastside Vancouver say about health and housing to each other, to members of their communities, to researchers, and to others? How do they understand relationships between health and housing? How do they describe their experiences? What can be learned by listening to their stories, attending to their words, and understanding their perspectives? What analyses do they offer? What possibilities do they see?" Dara Culhane coordinated the project, while Leslie Robertson, who worked intensively with community-based researchers, was primarily responsible for conducting ethnographic research and interviews.

In an attempt to make our research accountable to participants as well as to those whose lives may be affected by it, we followed a three-stage research process. In the first stage, researchers working with community partners prepared verbal and written reports and organized discussions. The ethnographic team transcribed audiotapes and returned transcripts to the woman interviewed. As they read over their words, some women found their stories uninteresting, some found them too revealing, many experienced discomfort, and most decided to remain anonymous, choosing to add their personal stories to a comprehensive and collective representation of issues facing women in Vancouver's Downtown Eastside. With their names and other personal identifiers removed, and confidentiality and anonymity guaranteed, most women who worked with the ethnographic team contributed their transcripts to the Health & Home database. Some, however, became very involved in the monthly meetings and worked to record their personal histories with the intention of eventual publication.

In the second stage of dissemination of Health & Home research, which is currently under way, summaries and analyses of responses to the structured interviews, transcripts of those open-ended discussions which were entered into the database, and other materials are being prepared in language and formats we hope will be accessible and useful to community organizations and advocates. Literature reviews, reports, and resources are available at http://www.sfu.ca/~fisls/health_home.htm. Finally, in the third stage, academic researchers will prepare articles for publication in scholarly journals and compile an edited volume of papers for publication by an academic press.

In Plain Sight emerged as a relatively autonomous and distinct project, developed from the work of the Health & Home Project's ethnographic team, predominately from those researchers working with women who were drug users and sex trade workers. In January 2003, Leslie contacted the women who had expressed a desire to publish their life stories early on in the research process, and who had worked to record their reflections for this book. As *In Plain Sight* unfolded, several women who had initially been involved dropped out. Some became ill. Several moved away from the Downtown Eastside and did not keep in touch with us. For a number of women, the force of events and crises in their lives, and the lives of people close to them, made it difficult for them to keep to researchers' schedules. A few women we were working with died. *In Plain Sight* represents a compilation and publication of interviews developed by seven women participants through processes explained in depth in the introduction.

APPENDIX 2: GLOSSARY OF TERMS AND SERVICES

Acid	Another term for LSD (lysergic acid diethylamide-25).
AIDS	Acquired Immune Deficiency Syndrome.
Aryan Nations	Extremist organization based on a belief in white supremacy and neo-Nazi ideologies.
Cap	Capsules.
Carries	Medication that clients take home and administer themselves.
Cellulitis	Infection of the skin and underlying tissues. commonly experienced by injection drug users.
Chicken	Slang term for overdosing (e.g., "doing the chicken").
Coconut	Slang term for cocaine users.
CPR	Cardio-pulmonary resuscitation.
Crack	Hard, crystalline form of cocaine that is broken into small pieces and then smoked or inhaled. Also known as "rock."
DD1	Dideoxyinosine, an anti-retroviral AIDS drug.
Disability Two	Social assistance for people with permanent disabilities. They receive $786 per month, medical and dental coverage, a maximum housing allowance of $325, a low-cost transit pass, and monthly earning exemptions of $300. As of October 2002 the provincial government required persons on DB II to apply for re-assessment, which could drop their benefits to $510 per month.
Dope sick	Ill from the physiological and psychological effects of withdrawal.
Dope simple	State of craving, withdrawal, or intoxication wherein people make unsafe/unsound decisions based on their need to obtain drugs.
Down	Heroin.
Eight-ball	3.5-gram measurement of cocaine or heroin.
Ensure	Nutritional supplement for maintaining or gaining weight.
Fixing	Injecting drugs.
Flagging	Drawing blood into the syringe to ensure the user has injected into a vein.
Flap	Small amounts of heroin and cocaine are sold in folded paper; also called "papers."
Freebase	To purify and strengthen cocaine by heating it, then smoking or inhaling it.
Front	To obtain drugs without paying for them at the time.

Gastown	A primarily commercial tourist district adjacent to the Downtown Eastside.
Harm reduction	A set of philosophies, strategies, and policies for reducing the physical and social harm associated with high-risk behaviours. Regarding drug use these include: safe injection sites, needle exchanges, methadone treatment, and the supervised prescription of heroin. Harm reduction seeks to prevent or minimize disease, death, incarceration, and stigmatization through interventions that enhance the quality of life for individuals and communities.
Hit	To find a vein to inject either yourself or someone else.
HIV	Human Immunodeficiency Virus.
Hoots	Smoking drugs.
IV	Intravenous.
John	Man who pays for sex.
K	Designates the purity level of heroin.
Lines	A way of snorting powdered cocaine.
MDA	Methylenedioxyamphetamine. Chemically related to mescaline and amphetamines.
Meds	Short for medications.
Mescaline	A hallucinogenic drug extracted from the peyote cactus.
Meth	(1) Methamphetamine, also called "speed," "crystal," and "crank." (2) short for methadone.
Methadone	Medically administered opiate used primarily to stabilize heroin addiction.
Ministry	Ministry of Children and Families.
Neuropathy	A common neurological disorder caused by diseases of the nerves or systemic illnesses.
No-go zone	A legal edict that prohibits people from being in an area where they have been known to conduct illegal activities. May have a time restriction attached.
OD	To overdose on drugs.
100 Block	The 100 block of West Hastings Street in the Downtown Eastside.
Packers	Person who holds drugs for the dealer in exchange for a commission of money or substances.
Paper	Small amounts of heroin and cocaine sold in folded paper, also called "flaps."
PCP	Phencyclidine, also called "angel dust," was developed in the 1950s as an anaesthetic and discontinued for human

use a decade later because of the side effects: agitation, delusions, and irrational behaviour.

Peelers	Capsules that contain morphine.
Powder	Powdered cocaine.
Regulars	Men who maintain long-term commercial relationships with women in the sex trade.
Rig	Syringe and needle for injecting drugs.
Rock	Single unit of crack cocaine. It has a hard, crystalline appearance and costs ten dollars.
Schedule C	Persons on Disability Two were eligible for extended health benefits under Schedule C that included $300 in addition to monthly support and shelter allowance. The provincial government cancelled the Monthly Health Allowance in October 2001.
Shoot	Inject.
SRO	Single-room occupancy hotel.
Staph	Infection caused by *staphylococcus aureus*; a common skin bacterium that enters the body through injecting or through cuts and abrasions.
Stashing	Hiding money and drugs in different places in case you are robbed.
Steers	Person who directs a buyer to a dealer in exchange for a commission of money or drugs.
Survival sex trade	Sex work conducted by impoverished, often drug-addicted women who work on the street where they receive less pay and often endure more dangerous working conditions than those who work through brothels and escort agencies.
TB	Tuberculosis.
Trannie	Transgendered or transsexual person.
Trick	Man who pays for sex.
Tweaking	Idiosyncratic behaviours that develop over the course of prolonged cocaine use.
Up	Cocaine or stimulants.
Whack	Injection of drugs.
Wired	Addicted to heroin.
Working girl	Woman who works in the sex trade.

ORGANIZATIONS, SERVICES, AND INSTITUTIONS

Al-Anon	Support for families and partners of alcoholics
ATIRA	Women's Resource Society
BCCW	Burnaby Correctional Centre for Women
Carnegie	Carnegie Centre
Crabtree	YWCA Crabtree Corner
DEYAS	Downtown Eastside Youth Action Society
GVMHS	Greater Vancouver Mental Health Society
Health Van	Downtown Eastside Health Outreach Van (DEYAS and Vancouver Native Health)
Kettle	Kettle Friendship Society
Kiwassa	Kiwassa Neighbourhood Services Association
MAT /DOT	Maximally Assisted Therapy / Directly Observed Therapy
MCF	Ministry of Children and Family Development
NA	Narcotics Anonymous
Oakalla	Oakalla Prison Farm (1912–1991)
PACE	Prostitution Alternatives Counselling Education
PEERS	Prostitutes Empowerment Education and Resource Society
PHN	PACE Health Network
Portland	Portland Hotel Society
PWN	Positive Women's Network
SAFER	Suicide Attempt, Follow-up, Education and Research (Vancouver Coastal Health Authority)
SARA	Sexual Abuse Recovery Anonymous
St.Paul's	Saint Paul's Hospital
St. James	Social assistance office.
Triage	Triage Emergency Services and Care Society
VANDU	Vancouver Area Network of Drug Users
VGH	Vancouver General Hospital
WISH	Women's Information Safe House Drop-In Centre
Women's Centre	Downtown Eastside Women's Centre
YWCA	Young Women's Christian Association

ACKNOWLEDGEMENTS

Many people, in many ways, have contributed to the development of this collection of stories. Both Leslie and Dara wish to particularly and sincerely thank Julie Cruikshank for giving of her time reading, commenting, and discussing several drafts, always with characteristic generosity, brilliance, and compassion. We are grateful to Joanne Richardson for her labour and commitment to editing earlier drafts of the manuscript. Joanne's contributions went far beyond the call of duty. Gary Fisher facilitated the final stages of editing and production with patience, insight, and good humour.

Leslie's acknowledgements: *In Plain Sight* took shape over the course of four years, and there are many to whom I owe thanks: Femke Van Delft listened her way through this project and I am grateful for our dialogues that crossed and re-crossed the thorny terrain of representation and aesthetics; she also lent her eyes to this book, photographing images for the cover. Mo Gaffney and Jesse Abel were generous readers, listeners, and discussants, who on several occasions offered thoughtful responses to complicated issues that arose during the process of editing and writing. Fellow researchers on the Health & Home Project—Dorothy Chunn, Denielle Elliot and Cathy Chabot—contributed edited interviews to this book; they read the stories and offered thoughtful comments.

Workers from several agencies encouraged women's participation in this work, always supporting their visions for social justice. The staff at the Ovaltine Café allowed us to over-stay on many occasions, providing a comfortable place to work out of the rain. Other residents in the Downtown Eastside generously offered insights into the relationships and realities that affect the public voice of street-involved women. Over these years, the humour and courage of Pawz, Laurie, Black Widow, Anne, Sarah, Dee, and Tamara were always evident, and working with them was always a pleasure.

Dara's acknowledgements: I thank my family and friends for their unfailing patience and support during the trials and tribulations of another project. Lori Gabrielson shared her inimitable insights and critiques gained from decades of living and working in and for the Downtown Eastside community. I thank her for her honesty and friendship over lo these many years. John Gilmore donated a writerly ear, editing, and detailed suggestions for revisions, many of which we did not take up, but all of which I appreciated.

None of these people is responsible, of course, for any of the content.